Profiles of Notable Missourians
For the Missouri Bicentennial

Thomas H. Olbricht

SULIS PRESS

An Imprint of Sulis International Press
Los Angeles | London

Published by Sulis Press
An imprint of Sulis International Press
Los Angeles and London
www.sulisinternational.com

Library of Congress Control Number: 2019941117
ISBN (print): 978-1-946849-42-7
ISBN (eBook): 978-1-946849-43-4

Contents

Chronological Sequence of Profiles

Dedicated to Richard and Jan Hughes,
consummate narrators and one-time Missourians.

Preface

I first got to know Tom Olbricht's writing because of a profile he wrote for Missouri Life magazine. I can't think of a higher compliment to this book than that I really wanted Missouri Life to publish it, not just because of the content—the famous Missourians—but also because Tom uses a friendly, conversational writing style that makes you want more. I also trusted his thorough research, seriously critical in these days of an internet full of information with all kinds of errors. It wasn't meant to be, for a variety of reasons, at the time that it needed to be published. I'm so thrilled that he quickly found another publisher.

This book about famous Missourians, or people who spent significant time here before moving on, by a Missourian, even though transplanted elsewhere now, with its fresh approach of combining his own reflections, memories, or surprising live connections with each is one will help any reader further appreciate Missouri's influence in the country, long ago, and still today.

I also believe it speaks volumes about Tom and the kind of person he is that he still invited me to write a preface. I am pleased that he proceeded with his inspiration for the book, and you will be surprised at many of the Missouri connections, from Stephen Austin to Sam Walton, or from Dred Scott through people like Dale Carnegie and Sinclair Lewis, all the way to Porter Wagoner. I am happy to recommend it.

—Danita Wood, Editor, *Missouri Life*

Introduction

In 2021, Missourians will celebrate the Bicentennial of their entry into the United States of America as the twenty-fourth state. The admission of Maine, the twenty-third state, occurred March 15, 1820. Maine and Missouri achieved statehood through the legendary Missouri Compromise brokered by the famous Kentucky senator, Henry Clay. The compromise addressed the balance of Slave and Free states in the Union. Maine was admitted as a Free State and Missouri as a Slave State. In 1821, twelve states were Free and twelve were Slave. It was understood at the time that these arrangements would continue westward, keeping the number of Free and Slave states evenly balanced. Racial status and distribution troubled the Congress of the United States for the next forty years and was finally resolved by the Civil War 1861-1865.

Through the two centuries of its statehood, prominent Americans have lived in or had ties with Missouri. Missourians will have not only statehood to celebrate but also the feats of several notable citizens. In this book, I set out details pertaining to thirty-four fellow Missourians. These well-known persons are distributed chronologically from the late seventeen hundreds into the twenty-first century. They are both male and female. They are both people of Color and White. Their contributions to humankind include art, athletics, entertainment, entrepreneurship, history, law, literature, the military, mining, music, politics, science, and theology.

I was born in Thayer, Missouri, on the Arkansas border, in 1929 and graduated from Thayer Elementary School 1943, and Alton High School in Missouri in 1947. I have lived in ten states and visited all fifty. I have been on six of the seven continents, and lived in three, only passing over Antarctica. Even though I haven't lived in Missouri for seventy years, I have always relished my Missouri heritage. I have been proud to say I am a Missourian even when people responded, "Oh you are from the Show-Me State!" Or they might ask, "Then you are as stubborn as a Missouri mule?"

In my book *Missouri Memories: 1943-1947*, I reflected on Missouri in World War II war times:

> I turned 12 the month before Pearl Harbor. Now the halcyon
> days of youth faded into oblivion. I quickly came of age. In an-
> other two years, I entered Alton, Missouri, High School in the

fall of 1943. The war raged on. The news of lost battles constantly bombarded the radio waves and the newsreels at our movie theatre. The invasion of Normandy Beach was still a year away. In the next two years, I learned with growing skill to navigate the far-reaching impact of war and in my final year of high school, an astounding peace. These years remain indelibly etched in my thoughts—momentous Missouri memories. These long months comprised my own boot camp; not for military service but for the battle of life[1].

I have more than portrayed the persons I have profiled. Anyone with competent internet search skills can access extensive information regarding all thirty-four persons under consideration, especially the sites of The State Historical Society of Missouri's "Historic Missourians" and "Wikipedia." I have brought my own experiences to bear in every case whether it is what I read growing up, saw as an adult, my own first-hand contact with the person under consideration, or the reports from my acquaintances who knew the notables personally. In this sense, these profiles are my own personal reminiscences of these thirty-four Missouri notables. The texts are interlaced with pictures so as to provide a visual narrative as well as a text depiction.

Congratulations on either being a Missourian or interested in our state and its people! We are a proud, and perhaps a stubborn lot. Our forebears have accomplished much in two hundred years. We anticipate that readers will come to know these notable Missourians better through the profiles and will empathize with us as we celebrate.

---

[1] *Missouri Memories: 1943-1947* (Eugene, Oregon: Wipf and Stock, 2016), 101.

1
Stephen F. Austin (1793-1836): Migrant Missourian Miner

What in common have Potosi, Missouri, and Austin, Texas? At first thought, almost nothing. Potosi, founded in 1773, has about 2,700 people. Austin, founded in 1839, is approaching 1,000,000. If the metropolitan areas are included, differences still persist. Potosi, in the St. Louis statistical region, is almost 3,000,000 in population while Austin is 2,000,000. What Potosi and Austin have in common is Stephen Fuller Austin (1793-1836), who mined lead in Potosi and played such a significant role in the founding of Texas that the state capitol was named for him.

Stephen F. Austin, 1840. Texas State Library and Archives Commission.

Migration to Missouri

Stephen F. Austin was born in Austinville, Virginia, a town founded by his father Moses Austin, located north of Charlotte, North Carolina. Moses and his brother Stephen owned and operated a lead mine nearby. As the price of lead deteriorated Moses pulled up stakes and moved his family and slaves by wagon train into Spanish Louisiana Territory near St. Louis, Missouri. They settled in the vicinity of the French Mine á Breton, that possessed rich deposits of the lead, but also silver and copper. Soon thereafter Moses founded the town of Potosi which in Spanish means "treasure" and was the name of a celebrated silver mine in Bolivia. In 1800, France received the Louisiana territory from Spain by treaty, and then, in 1803, Thomas Jefferson negotiated the famous Louisiana Purchase with Napoleon. The northern part of the purchase was soon designated the Missouri Territory. The Potosi mine was successful and Moses became wealthy. For a time after 1805 the Austin's mines shipped out 800,000 tons of lead a year. He also founded Herculaneum on the Mississippi River where he located a technically advanced lead smelter

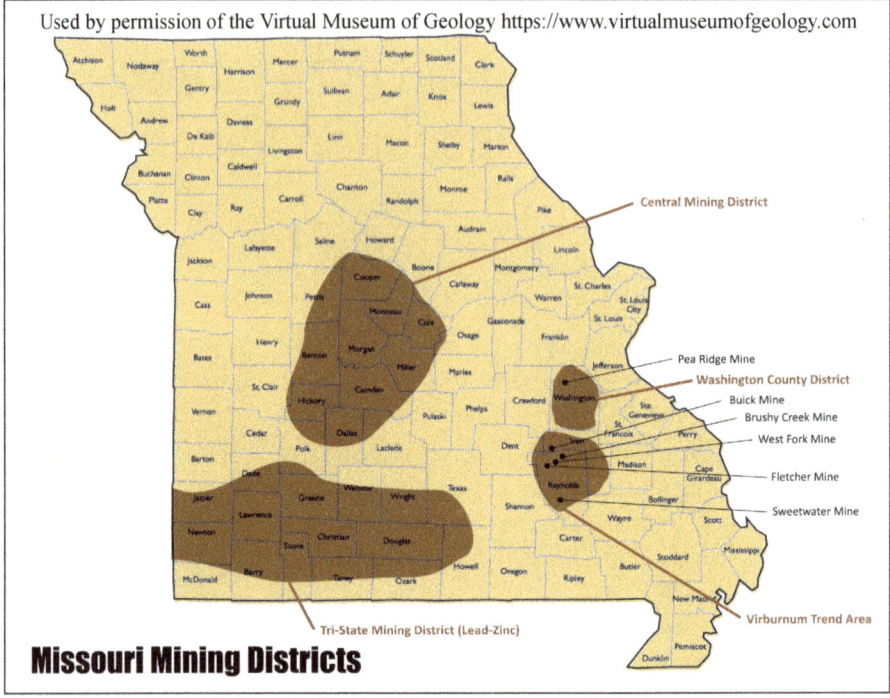

Used by permission of the Virtual Museum of Geology https://www.virtualmuseumofgeology.com

Central Mining District

Pea Ridge Mine
Washington County District
Buick Mine
Brushy Creek Mine
West Fork Mine

Fletcher Mine

Sweetwater Mine

Virburnum Trend Area

Tri-State Mining District (Lead-Zinc)

Missouri Mining Districts

and docks for shipping. Lead was in demand during the War of 1812 but unfortunately, a British naval blockade prohibited shipment to the battle sites.

Coming to the conclusion that Stephen had exceptional capability for learning, Moses sent his son to Bacon Academy in Colchester, Connecticut, and then to Transylvania University in Lexington, Kentucky. Stephen graduated from Transylvania in 1810; a decade later Jefferson Davis, President of the Confederacy, attended Transylvania. Even while in school during breaks Stephen helped his father operate a store, and upon graduation assisted him in managing the mines. Missouri was organized as a territory in 1812 and the capital of the territory, then the state, was located in St. Charles from 1813-1826. In 1813, at age 20, Stephen was elected to the Missouri Territorial Legislature and each year afterward until 1819. He also served as an adjunct commissioner in the Missouri Militia. Both Moses and Stephen were instrumental in creating the Bank of St. Louis, but because of declining lead prices, the bank failed. Moses' financial situation became increasingly precarious. Feeling boxed in by debt in Missouri, Moses Austin, ever the entrepreneur, anticipated new opportunities in the developing Texas territory and moved to Texas in 1820, a year before Missouri attained statehood.

Mining Lead in Missouri

French explorers in the 1720s mined the first lead in Missouri in the region around Potosi and Park Hills. The mines tended to be shallow and often one miner operations. The Austins mined deeper, employing a crew of miners including African-American slaves. It was not until the 1850s that lead and zinc mining commenced in the tri-state area around Joplin. In the Lake of the Ozarks region, mining commenced in the 1830s but didn't produce the tonnage of the other two regions.

The area around Potosi, identified as the old lead belt, has been a major world producer of lead. The tonnage over two centuries has exceeded 8.5 million. The old belt continued to produce around Leadwood and Park Hills (originally Flat River) until 1972. At that time on the west at Viburnam and south, a newer area is still active contributing lead to battery manufacturing. It is believed that lead can be found southward from Viburnum even into the Irish Wilderness in northeast Oregon County. The wilderness is designated Irish because of the failed effort of a Roman Catholic priest to estab-

Oscar Berninghaus mural depicts early lead mining in Washington County, Missouri.

lish a community of his fellow countrymen. A sizeable percentage of the area south of Viburnum is in the Mark Twain National Forest and that in turn constrains permission to explore for ores.

In the early 1960s my mother, after having completed a master's degree in elementary education, took a position as a first grade teacher in Leadwood, Missouri. She taught there until mandatory retirement at age seventy in 1968. On family visits, we learned about the lead mining industry which was still quite active. We had four children who always needed something to do. My father, who was in his late seventies, and I took the

5

older kids to the tall mounds of lead ore chat. We climbed around and slid to the bottom. It was great fun. At that time those we knew were little concerned about lead poisoning. We visited a church in Flat River and there met a man who was a high-level manager in the lead miles. I talked with him at some length. He spoke of the electric trains in underground tunnels for hauling ore. Above three hundred miles of track existed. He reported that one could go from Leadwood all the way to Potosi eleven miles northwest. He said he would be glad to take me on an underground train excursion, but I was never able to manage an appropriate occasion.

Texas Migration

In October of 1820, Moses Austin headed to Texas to make a new start. He proposed to the governor of the Texas Territory that he be permitted to settle 300 families in the state from San Antonio, south to the Gulf of Mexico. Texas belonged to Spain from 1690 to 1821. Texas came under the Mexican flag in 1821, the year in which Mexico secured independence from Spain. Texans fought for independence from Mexico which they obtained in 1836. The state was the Republic of Texas until 1845 at which time it was admitted to the United States. Austin's petition was finally granted by the governor, but before heading back to Missouri to move his family, he came down with pneumonia. He never fully recovered, died June 10, 1821, and was buried in Potosi, Missouri. Before his death, he implored Stephen F. Austin to assume the challenge of moving three hundred families to Texas.

Stephen F. Austin, in the meanwhile, settled in Arkansas, which achieved statehood in 1836, and bought land where the new capital in the Little Rock was to be located, but he was deprived of his purchase by a court decision. He also ran for the territorial congress but lost. He considered studying law and moved to New Orleans. While Stephen was still in Louisiana, his father died. Stephen was reluctant to accept the Texas proposition, but his mother convinced him by letter to proceed. He rode his horse to San Antonio, arriving on August 12, 1821. The grant met resistance from the nascent Mexican government, so Stephen F. traveled to Mexico City. The petition was finally granted in 1823 and ultimately approved in 1825 so that the families began to settle on their large acreages.

Texas achieved independence from Mexico in 1836. With some hesitation, Austin ran for president but was defeated by Sam Houston. Houston proposed that Austin accept the secretary of state position, which he did. On December 27, 1836, Stephen F. Austin died of pneumonia.

Stephen F. Austin is widely memorialized in Texas. Not only is the state Capitol named Austin but also a county, and a university, Stephen F. Austin State University (1923), Nacogdoches, Texas. Our granddaughter, Teysha (resembling Tejas), was born in Texas and, along with her husband Turner Vinson, graduated from the University. Austin College in Sherman is also named for the Potosi, Missouri, migrant.

2
Ma Barker (1873-1935): Southern Missouri's Great Depression Gang

The most famous Missouri gang was that of Jesse and Frank James who terrorized Mid-Western populations in the chaotic era from 1868 to 1882 following the Civil War. The end came when Robert Ford, a gang member, shot Jesse James in the back. The James Gang has been memorialized in ballads, poems, and motion pictures.

The financial uncertainties of the great depression produced another surge of criminal gangs including those of Al Capone, John Dillinger, Baby Face Nelson, Machine Gun Kelly, Bonnie Parker and

Ma Barker. Unknown photographer and date.

Clyde Barrow (who lived in Joplin, Missouri for a time), and Pretty Boy Floyd, who was charged with the killing of law enforcement officers in Kansas City. To this list may be added a notorious gang—the Barker-Karpis Gang, that terrorized South Central Missouri and elsewhere in several Midwestern states in the early 1930s.

The Gang

The Barker-Karpis Gang was sometimes designated the Ma Barker Gang. Much speculation persisted as the exact role played by this unconventional mother figure. According to J. Edgar Hoover, Director of the FBI (1924-1972) Ma was "the most vicious, dangerous and resourceful criminal brain of the last decade." Others cast doubt on her role as the strategist of the gang, claiming that Hoover advanced his sensational depiction to justify Ma's death at the hands of the FBI in 1935. According to gang member Alvin "Creepy" Karpis, Ma Barker couldn't even plan breakfast.

Ma Barker

Arizona Donnie Clark Barker (1873-1935) was born in Ash Grove, Missouri, ten miles northwest of Springfield. The farm where she lived is now the Staton Dairy Farm. Growing up she was called Arrie or Kate. She married George Barker (1868-1941) in 1892. One of her memorable experiences as a child was seeing Jesse James ride through town. Ma was brought up among those criminally disposed. She raised her four sons in a tar paper shack in Aurora, Missouri, east of Joplin, and played the role of a distraught mother when as teenagers they were jailed for robbery and other misdemeanors. The family moved to Webb City in 1904 and to Tulsa, Oklahoma in 1915. George disassociated himself from the family and moved back to Joplin, worked in a filling station, and rejected the outlaw life of his sons. Ma liked finer things and bought jewelry and expensive clothes with money provided by her sons' robberies.

The Ma Barker Gang came into being in 1931, but the crimes of the Barker sons went back as early as 1910 in the region around Joplin, then later in Oklahoma and Kansas. The oldest son was Herman, born in 1893. He killed himself in 1927 to avoid arrest. The second was Lloyd, who lived the longest (1897-1949). After a later successful life as a chef, he was gunned down by his wife. Lloyd was arrested but declared insane.

Thayer, Missouri. Picture from Olbricht collection.

The third son, Arthur "Doc" (1899-1939) died in Alcatraz trying to escape, and Fred (1901-1935), mom's favorite, was in the Kansas State Prison from 1927-1931, where he met Alvin "Creepy" Karpis and brought him into the Gang. Karpis was born in Montreal, Canada, but raised in Topeka, Kansas. There were other members of the gang, and according to later reports they murdered more than ten people and stole or extorted a ransom of more than three million dollars.

Thayer, Missouri

In September of 1931 Ma Barker, her lover Arthur Dunlop, Fred Barker, and "Creepy" Karpis rented a farmhouse two miles east of Thayer, Missouri. Ma had grown weary of constant grilling by the police in Tulsa regarding the activities of her sons. She wanted to move to a place where the family was unknown and where backcountry roads would provide convenient escape routes. Dunlop didn't get along well with Fred and "Creepy," but they tolerated him. Dunlop misled area residents to believe that he was a wealthy Oklahoma oilman and had retired. From their Thayer base, Fred and Creepy proceeded to rob area banks, the first ones north of Thayer in Mountain View and Birch Tree, Missouri.

Killing Sheriff C. Roy Kelly

The most serious crime committed by Fred Barker and Alvin Creepy Karpis up to 1931 was killing the Howell County Sheriff in West Plains, Missouri, 25 miles northwest of Thayer, December 19, 1931. On December 17, Fred and Creepy robbed McCallon Clothing Store in West Plains of expensive men's wear worth $2000. Two days later Fred and Creepy returned to West Plains planning to rob the bank. Their expensive blue DeSoto sedan needed two tires fixed, so they pulled into Davidson Motor Company. The owner, Carac Davidson, noticed that their clothes matched those stolen from McCallon, so he quietly walked across the street to call McCallon on the phone. When McCallon arrived, Kelly stepped out of the post office. C. Roy Kelly was a well-liked elected sheriff born in Van Buren, MO east of West Plains in 1885. He and his family had lived in Springfield and Mountain View. Kelly walked to his car, took out his gun and then entered the garage to question Fred and Creepy. Kelly reached to open the thieves' car door. Shots rang out, and Kelly was dead. Barker fled on foot. Karpis tore out of the garage, tires squealing and disappeared. State lawmen arrived to help search for the car and soon discovered the men were headed for Thayer. A group of hunters accidentally found the car with bullet holes in the back. The officers checked the license plates and learned that the car belonged to Alvin "Creepy" Karpis. The lawmen then found that Mrs. Arthur Dunlop was actually Ma Barker. They went to the farm, but when they got there, the Gang had fled. They had shrewdly planted devices that warned them in advance of the approaching lawmen.

The Barker-Karpis Gang eventually relocated to St. Paul, Minnesota. At that time, several outlaws lived in the St. Paul, openly protected by bribes they handed to the local law officials. The Gang continued to operate, kidnaping William Hamm of the Hamm Brewing Company and extorting $100,000 in ransom money, and Edward Bremer, the scion of a wealthy banking family, raking in $200,000. Finally, in 1935, FBI officials discovered that Fred and Ma Barker were living in Ocklawaha, Florida. The officers surrounded the house and after a four-hour shoot-out—Ma Barker manning a machine gun—the shots ceased. Upon entering the house, the FBI discovered Ma and her son Fred bullet-ridden and dead.

Combatting Robbers

I was born in Thayer, Missouri, and was two years old when the Barker-Karpis Gang operated from their rented house. My Grandfather, T. Shelt Taylor, owned a Standard Oil gas station-grocery store on U.S. Highway 63. He had a burglar alarm on the door and windows, and the alarm sounded in his bedroom about a hundred fifty feet away. Since money was so scarce, break-ins were common. Granddad slept with a loaded pistol on a table by his bed. I slept in a second-floor bedroom overlooking the highway, and I could see the store driveway. Grandpa said he never wanted to kill or wound anyone, and in fact, he wasn't a very good shot with the pistol. If the alarm went off, he ran out the front door, somewhat hidden from the store by porch pillars, and fired the pistol into the air. More than once I was awakened by hearing a shot, then squealing tires as the thieves sped away. We went down to the store and usually found signs of efforts to jimmy the door or a window. I don't recall that

Picture from Olbricht collection.

Grandfather ever lost anything from within the store in those years, but sometimes used tires that were left outside were stolen. After the attempted break-ins occurred, I slept fitfully. I was afraid that Grandpa, or even I, might be injured. We heard various stories about gangs roaming the country, sometimes wounding or killing those they attempted to rob. The Barker-Karpis Gang was a vivid memory to the adults of my extended family.

A movie, "Bloody Mama," was released by Robert Corman in 1970 with Shelley Winters as Ma Barker, Robert De Niro as Lloyd Barker, and Michael Fox as Dr. Roth. Howard Kazanjian and Chris Enss published *Ma Barker: America's Most Wanted Mother* in 2016.

3

Thomas Hart Benton (1782-1856): A Missouri Senator and the Winning of the West

Horace Greeley, the editor of the *New York Post* at the end of the Civil War in 1865, capitalized on the slogan, "Go west, young man!" Many American families took Greeley seriously and headed west on wagon trails and river barges. Some, especially early Missouri settlers, preceded Greeley's charge by several decades. Among the migrants was Thomas Hart Benton (1782-1858), who became a celebrated first Missouri Senator.

Oil portrait of Senator Benton at National Portrait Gallery in Washington, D.C. by Ferdinand Thomas Lee Boyle (1820 - 1906) c. 1861.

Early Years

Thomas Hart Benton was born in Harts Mill, North Carolina. He came from a family of wealthy landowner lawyers. He studied at the University of North Carolina, but in 1799 dropped out to manage the family estate. Early in the 1800s, under the wishes of his mother, he moved the extended family to the region of Nashville, Tennessee, to establish a plantation on a 40,000-acre tract. He continued his legal studies and was admitted to the Tennessee Bar in 1805 and in 1909 served a term in the Tennessee State Senate. He was attracted to Jeffersonian Democracy and was an avid supporter of Andrew Jackson. During the War of 1812, Jackson made Benton his aide-de-camp, with a commission as a lieutenant colonel. In 1815 Thomas Hart Benton moved his family and slaves to a Missouri territory estate and settled in St. Louis for the rest of his life, except when the United States Senate and Congress were in session.

St. Louis may have been far enough West for Benton personally. But he was of the opinion that the United States should acquire territory all the way to the Pacific Ocean and initiate a significant impact all around the Asian Pacific Rim. He was a major proponent of Manifest Destiny and was enamored with an avowed superiority of Anglo-Saxon, Western European Civilization and its westward movement. He believed that homesteading acts and the building of railroads were prerequisite for opening up the vast western regions in North America. Benton pursued his commitments with great ardor in the Senate and Congressional Chambers for the rest of his career.

The Legislator

In St. Louis, Benton practiced law and edited the *Missouri Territory,* the second major newspaper printed west of the Mississippi River. Missouri was approved for statehood in 1820 by the Missouri Compromise, in which Missouri entered as a slave state and Maine as a free state. In 1821 Missouri voted its first senators into office, and one of the two was Thomas Hart Benton. Benton served in the Senate from 1821 to 1851, thirty years, that is, six terms. Thomas Hart became the chief Senate supporter of Andrew Jackson who was president of the United States from 1829 to 1837. Benton began to lose favor with Missouri voters when he opposed slavery after the Mexican War. He served one term in the United States House of Representatives 1852 to 1854. In 1821, Benton married Elizabeth McDowell, born in Virginia. The Bentons had six children, among them a daughter Jesse Benton, who married presidential candidate John C. Frémont, the 1856 Republican nominee.

Manifest Destiny

Several early Americans championed the western expansion of Mediterranean, Anglo-Saxon Civilization, as did Cotton Mather in colonial days. Benjamin Franklin, in a 1730 Boston News-Letter, printed a couplet said to have been cut into a rock at Plymouth, Massachusetts, "The Eastern World enslav'd, it's Glory ends: And Empire rises where the Sun descends." A hundred years later Senator Thomas Hart Benton clearly expressed the same sentiment (1846):

> The Red race has disappeared from the Atlantic coast; the tribes that resisted civilization met extinction. This is a cause of lamentation with many. For my part, I cannot murmur at what seems to be the effect of divine law. I cannot repine that this Capitol has replaced the wigwam—this Christian people, replaced the

savages—white matrons, the red squaws…Civilization, or extinction, has been the fate of all people who have found themselves in the trace of the advancing Whites, and civilization, always the preference of the Whites, has been pressed as an object, while extinction has followed as a consequence of its resistance…[1]

Benton insisted, however, that oceans should not impede the march of the United States flag, that American influence must likewise cross the Pacific.

The sun of civilization must shine across the sea; socially and commercially the van of the Caucasians, and the rear of the Mongolians must intermix. They must talk together, and trade together, and marry together…Moral and intellectual superiority will do the rest; the White race will take the ascendant, elevating what is susceptible of improvement-wearing out what is not… And thus the youngest people, and the newest land, will become the reviver and the regenerator of the oldest….[2]

Homestead Act

For Caucasian Americans to win the west, Benton contended that a suitable homesteading policy was imperative. He opposed land speculation because, in his judgment, the outcome was that large tracks of land came under the control of a few, and failed to encourage white settlers to populate the west. Benton authored the first Homestead Act for the Democratic Party, but he was unable to secure its enactment. He proposed that 160 acres of land be given to homesteaders. For them to "prove up," it was necessary that they build a dwelling, arrange for water by spring or well, and live on the land for five years. Benton insisted on benefiting the common people, not just the few.

Though Benton's bill nearly passed both Houses, it was regularly opposed by congressmen from southern states who correctly perceived that western expansion would increase the number of free territories. After the southern states seceded from the Union, a homestead act was passed in 1862, and President Abraham Lincoln signed the bill. Both African-Americans and women were permitted to file for homesteads.

---

[1] Theodore Roosevelt, Thomas Hart Benton (Boston: Houghton, Mifflin, 1890), p. 347.

[2] Congressional Globe, 29:1 (1846), 917-18.

The Railroads

Thomas Hart Benton became an early advocate of railroads, even including a transcontinental line because rail transportation would attract and benefit new western settlers. The first steam trains operated in England by 1825. The Baltimore and Ohio Railroad launched the first passenger and freight line in the United States in 1827. The lines first steam engine arrived two years later with Peter Cooper's "Tom Thumb." That was the beginning of a half-century of resolute rail construction. Not only did the trains transport pioneers westward, even more important was the manner in which they enabled the westerners to ship their products to more lucrative eastern markets including grain, hogs, cattle, sheep, hides, and bleached buffalo bones.

Benton pushed railroads in the Senate even before they were operative in Missouri. The first Missouri railroad, the Pacific Railroad (later Missouri Pacific) began in 1849, charted to connect St. Louis with points west. The name expressed the hope that it would run all the way to the Pacific Ocean. The first trains of this line ran in 1852. It was not until after the Civil War was over in 1865 that the track finally reached Kansas City. For the next two decades, progress was unprecedented. By the middle 1880s trains were running in my hometown, Thayer, Missouri, through Springfield to Kansas City and southeast through Memphis to Birmingham. The line was the St. Louis-San Francisco, commonly designated the "Frisco." Thayer was a "railroad town," with a roundhouse and repair shop. At the height of railway transportation, the Frisco employed more than 400 Thayer area workers.

Benton was a major congressional supporter of a transcontinental railroad. Popular President Theodore Roosevelt (1901-1909) published an 1887 biography of Thomas Hart Benton. He wrote that Benton,

> ...would naturally support the proposal to build a Pacific Railroad, and accordingly, he argued for it at great length and with force and justice, at the same time opposing the propositions to build northern and southern trans-continental roads as substitutes for the proposed central route.[3]

During the Civil War the Central Pacific Railroad started laying track eastward from the Pacific Ocean, and after a time employed Chinese laborers as tunnel diggers. The Union Pacific pushed out of Omaha, Nebraska, utilizing a huge contingent of Irish immigrants. The feat was extraordinary requiring long grades, bridges across major streams and tunnels in the mountains. The national imagination was captured May 10, 1869, when the last golden spike for holding the rail in place was driven in Promontory, Utah.

Completion of the Transcontinental Railroad. Promontory, Utah.

---

[3] Theodore Roosevelt, Thomas Hart Benton (Boston: Houghton, Mifflin, 1890), p. 347.

Thomas Hart Benton was one of eight United States Senators profiled in John F. Kennedy's *Profiles in Courage* (1956). Both Thomas Hart and Elizabeth Benton are interred in the Bellefontaine Cemetery on West Florissant Avenue in St. Louis, Missouri.

Statue Harriet Hosmer. Erected in 1868. Picture by Whitebox (Aug 8, 2007).

4
George Caleb Bingham (1811-1879): Missouri River Master Painter

Missouri has not been the home of many internationally known painters. But two come to mind, Thomas Hart Benton (1889-1971) of Neosho and Kansas City and George Caleb Bingham (1811-1879) of Arrow Rock and Independence. In this vignette, I will placard George Caleb Bingham. I first became aware of Bingham through my friend Paul C. Nagel who published, *George Caleb Bingham: Missouri's Famed Painter and Forgotten Politician* (2005). Nagel also published, *Missouri: A History* (1977).

Self-Portrait of the Artist. c. 1834-1835.

The Move to Missouri

Bingham was born in 1811 in Augusta County, Virginia, northwest of Richmond on the West Virginia border, the second of seven children. His father lost most of his property to cover a friend's debts, so in 1819 the family headed to Missouri by wagon train, settling in Franklin just north of the Missouri River from Boonville. After a major flood, the town was rebuilt on a higher level and renamed New Franklin. The town was the end of the Santa Fe Trail and of significance when the Binghams arrived. Bingham's father founded an Inn and tobacco factory, and his mother opened the first school for girls west of the Mississippi.

George showed a precocious interest in art and drew on whatever surface available; fence posts, barn sides, scrap paper, and firewood. In 1820 a nationally known painter, Chester Harding, who sometimes lived in St. Louis, came to Boonville to paint Daniel Boone, the year of Boone's death. Harding's is the only known portrait painted while Boone was still alive. After watching Harding paint, Bingham aspired to become a portrait artist. Even though he painted several portraits, Bingham became famous because of his Missouri River scenes. Below is his painting, "Wood Boat."

The Wood-Boat. Oil on canvas. 1850.

"The Wood-Boat" tells a simple, straightforward story. Painted in 1850 it was a time in which travel on the Missouri River was at its heights. Missouri railroads were almost twenty years in the future. Most river travel upstream was by steamboat. Steamboats burned wood in order to produce steam. If no other source of wood was available, steamboats docked and the captains sent crew members to scavenge for fuel. It was much to the advantage of the captains, however, to purchase already solid cut and split wood. Entrepreneurs in the small river towns soon met the challenge. They loaded wood on river barges and waited in daylight hours for the appearance of a steamboat. In this painting, the river with its high banks is in the background. Behind the men are stacks of cut wood. They wait expectantly for a steamboat plying up the river, waving with a smile on their face anticipating a successful sale.

The contours of the painting are clear, but the sky seems to be approaching twilight. The woodcutters propose to load the steamboat, and both will tie up for the night. The colors are vivid and varied but blend well with the landscape. For any traveler on the Missouri, the painting represented a recurrent experience. It also resonates for those who fantasize about what it is like to live in the interior.

A Portrait Artist

In 1823 George's father died of malaria. Because of unpaid bills, his mother moved the family across the river to Arrow Rock and continued operating her school. George helped both on the farm and at school. After a time, and for the next five years, Jesse Green, a Methodist minister, tutored George in cabinet making. At seventeen, George moved to

Portrait of Vinnie Ream (1846-1914). c. 1876.
Wisconsin Historical Museum.

Boonville and apprenticed to Justinian Williams, also a Methodist minister and cabinetmaker. By woodworking and Biblical study George enriched his artistic and moral sensibilities. Bingham entertained becoming a lawyer and a preacher even fulfilling preaching engagements under the tutelage of the two ministers, but in a later meeting with Harding decided to take up portrait painting. After painting portraits for some of his friends and receiving their commendation, George gained confidence and soon traveled to other towns in Missouri. By 1833, when he was 22, George earned enough money to devote full time to painting.

In 1834, while painting in Columbia, Missouri, Bingham met James S. Rollins, an attorney and politician. They struck up a friendship that continued for the rest of their lives. Rollins helped Bingham financially and became his mentor. In 1838, seeking greater insight into painting George traveled to Philadelphia and New York so as to study art in the museums and galleries. He especially focused on paintings depicting scenes from everyday life. Bingham returned to Missouri with newly acquired skills and an enlarged vision of what he would put on his canvases. His immediate experiences consisted of life on the Missouri River and he proceeded to depict these in a dramatic manner. By 1845, the landscapes became his forte, and he inaugurated a copious artistic output enhancing his national reputation. He also depicted scenes of frontier social and political life.

"Family Life on the Frontier." Oil on canvas. c. 1845.
New Orleans Museum of Art.

Travels in Europe

In later years Bingham fulfilled a long time dream to scrutinize European art. He moved to Europe in 1856 with his second wife, Eliza, and young daughter. They rented rooms and spent several months in Paris where George frequented the Louvre Museum of art and intensely studied the old masters. After Paris, they took up residency in Düsseldorf, Germany, where Bingham became involved in the famed School of Painting. The Düsseldorf School emphasized hard-edged and meticulous lines, a style which Bingham embraced. The most prominent artist of the School was Emanuel Leutze, famous for his 1851 painting of Washington crossing the Delaware. Bingham completed commissions from the Missouri State Legislature, as well as independent paintings.

Bingham the Politician

In 1848, Bingham entered Missouri politics, having been elected to the state legislature as a Saline County representative. In June 1852 he represented Missouri's eighth district at the Whig National Convention. Bingham served as a Civil War captain in the northern Volunteer Reserve Corps. Missouri was forced to set up a provisional government during the war, and Bingham served as state treasurer from 1862 to 1865. In 1874, Bingham was appointed the president of the Kansas City Board of police commissioners, and the board appointed the first police chief in the city. In 1875, he became Missouri's adjutant general. Bingham also served on the Independence, Missouri, district school board, and a Middle School was named for him.

Toward the End

At the end of his life, Bingham was appointed the first professor of Art at the University of Missouri. A major exhibit of Bingham's works was arranged at the St. Louis Art Museum in 1934. George Caleb Bingham is lauded as one of the major United States Artists. Bingham made a commitment to art early in his career. In 1837 he wrote his friend James Rollins, "There is no honorable sacrifice which I would not make to attain eminence in the art of which I have devoted myself."

5

Albert E. Brumley (1905-1979): Missouri Gospel Musician

The names of rock stars, country western singers, Irish tenors, and symphony directors are burned indelibly in our memories. Songwriters, however, are typically unknown, except in the music venues for which they write. The name Albert E. Brumley (1905-1977), a long-time resident of Powell, Missouri, may be unfamiliar. His Gospel songs, however, are heard throughout the world in significant settings.

Albert E. Brumley.

We spent a sabbatical in eastern Massachusetts in 1975 and 1976. We attended a Boston Pops Concert, with Arthur Fiedler conducting, at the Esplanade on the Charles River in Boston. That night, the Pops played Albert E. Brumley's often recorded song, "I'll Fly Away" (published in 1932). That caught me by surprise since I grew up singing that gospel hymn in Oregon Country Missouri, in the middle of the state, on the Arkansas border. I later discovered that in 1966 Fiedler produced "The Pops Goes Country," with Chet Atkins playing his guitar and "I'll Fly Away" a featured song.

About ten years ago I watched Garrison Keillor's, "The Prairie Home Companion." The show featured a quartet dressed in polyester 1970s suits. One of their songs was Albert E. Brumley's, "Turn Your Radio On," first published in 1938. Albert E. Brumley's gospel songs have reached multitudes across continents and oceans. A recording of "I'll Fly Away" by the Chuck Wagon Gang in 1949 sold over a million copies. The Smithsonian Institute declared that Albert Brumley was the greatest writer of Gospel music prior to World War II.

Early Years

Albert Brumley was born in Spiro, Oklahoma, in what was then Indian Territory, southwest of Fort Smith, Arkansas. His parents later bought a farm on the Arkansas border farther south in Rock Island, Oklahoma. Music engulfed young Brumley's life. His father was a noted fiddler. Even while in high school Brumley attended shaped-note singing schools which in turn whetted his appetite for county gospel music. At age twenty he proceeded to enroll at the Hartford Music Institute of E. M. Bartlett (1885-1941) even taking his board and room at Bartlett's house in Hartford, Arkansas, south of Fort Smith. He studied at the Institute until 1931. Bartlett's Institute became famous in southern gospel circles and Bartlett himself published such songs of prominence as "Victory in Jesus" and "Just a Little While to Stay Here." Brumley sang bass with the Hartford quartet and was in demand as a pianist and as a teacher for singing schools.

Powell, Missouri

Old Homeplace of Albert And Goldie Brumley.

In 1931, Brumley married Goldie Schell who lived in Powell, Missouri, south of Joplin and just north of Bentonville, Arkansas—Walmart headquarters. The Brumley's bought a house in Powell and lived there until Brumley's death in 1977. After his death, a major throughway in Powell was named the Albert Brumley Memorial Highway. The Brumleys raised their six children, five boys and a girl, in the Powell hamlet. The Brumleys were members of the Church of Christ in Powell, Missouri.

Brumley wrote for the Stamps-Baxter Music Company in Dallas, for Hartland, and also started the Albert E. Brumley and Sons Music Company in 1943. The Brumleys purchased the Harford Company in 1948, thus acquiring the copyright to some of Albert's own best-known songs.

In his lifetime Brumley published over 800 Gospel songs including, "I'll Fly Away," "Jesus Hold My Hand" (1933), "If We Never Meet Again the Side of Heaven" (1945), "I Will Meet You in the Morning" (1936), "Salvation Has Been Brought Down" (1940), "He Set Me Free" (1939), "I know Somebody's Listening," (1936) "This World is not my Home" (1937), and "Turn Your Radio On."

Several well-known stars have recorded Albert Brumley compositions, including Merle Haggard, George Jones, Glen Campbell, Crystal Gayle, Chet Atkins, Porter Wagoner, and Hank Williams. Hank Williams negotiated with Brumley to employ a version of the musical notation for "He Set Me Free" in his hit song, "I Saw the  Light," (1948). "I'll Fly Away" has been sung in several movies and television shows including Robert Duvall's "The Apostle" and the 2001 frequently awarded movie, "O Brother, Where Art Thou?"

Brumley launched the "Sundown to Sunup Gospel Sing" in Springdale, Arkansas, in the late 1900s. The Sing continued in Fayetteville until 2001 at which time it moved to Lebanon, Missouri, as a four-day festival designated "The Albert E. Brumley Gospel Music Sing." In 2016 the Gospel Music Sing was relocated to Tulsa, Oklahoma. Should the Sing be held in 2018, it will be the 50th Sing. From 1989 to 2003 the Brumleys produced the Brumley Family Music Show in Branson, Missouri.

Brumley has been inducted into the Nashville Songwriters Hall of Fame, Gospel Music Hall of Fame, and the Oklahoma Music Hall of Fame. Albert E. Brumley, Jr. became a recognized performer and songwriter. Tom Brumley was a celebrity steel guitar player with Buck Owens (1963-1969) and Ricky Nelson (1969-1981) during the same period for ten years. Bill and Bob Brumley have been involved in the Hartford Music Company. Bob Brumley in recent years became the sole owner of the company.

According to Brumley's son Albert E. Brumley, Jr., his father worked meticulously over his songs.

> Brumley would often spend years tinkering with a song, looking
> for just the right combination of words and music that would
> reach out and touch his audience. The Brumley kids would often

hear him pecking at the piano late at night in his lifelong quest to perfect yet another song. By the end of his life, Brumley had written over 700 songs, many of them timeless standards—from the starkness of "Rank Strangers" and "Nobody Answered Me" to the sweetness of "I'll Meet You in The Morning,l to the unstoppable bounce of "Turn Your Radio On." James R. Goff Jr., in his book *A History Of Southern Gospel,* observed that Brumley transformed earlier country gospel styles to both sentimental and upbeat songs which resonated with an audience trying to adjust to the pace and technology of the twentieth century.[1]

Growing up with Brumley Songs

In the Churches of Christ I attended in the days of my youth in Thayer, Missouri, and Mammoth Spring, Arkansas, we often sang Albert Brumley songs. We heard his repertory on the radio sung by Gospel quartets. I recall being introduced to "If We Never Meet Again This Side of Heaven" soon after it was published as well as "I'll Meet you in the Morning." In those years women trios were popular such as the Andrews Sisters. The Mammoth congregation had a Frazier Sisters Trio that sang at area gatherings. I recall especially their version of "Jesus Hold My Hand." Theirs was a memorable rendition.

In the 1970s, I went with my uncle Cleo Taylor, who loved Sunday afternoon singings, to the Hickory Grove Church of Christ at a Y-junction north of Alton, Missouri, near the famous Greer Spring. After we arrived, we discovered that the songs led that day were all, at the request of the leaders, written by Albert E. Brumley. Several copies of a collection of Brumley's songs were distributed to those present. The request was unusual since normally little attention was paid to those who wrote the songs. Typically tunes were selected because the song leaders liked them.

For many, the Gospel songs of Albert E. Brumley elicit precious memories of a by-gone era. Albert Brumley died in Springfield and is buried in the Fox Church of Christ Cemetery near Powell, Missouri. He died November 15, 1977.

---

[1] http://nodepression.com/album-review/albert-e-brumley-jr-36-greatest-gospel-memories-loving-tribute-albert-e-brumley; James R. Goff, Jr., *Close Harmony: A History of Southern Gospel* (Chapel Hill: The University of North Carolina Press, 2002).

6
Dale Carnegie (1888-1955): The Missouri Motivator

When I was a student in the Speech Department at the University of Iowa, from 1951 to 1954, working toward a doctorate, the major ridicule for someone in our profession was directed at Dale Carnegie. Regardless, likely more persons around the globe were involved in Dale Carnegie training programs than those in all the speech courses of universities and colleges combined. Academic speech professors considered Carnegie's approach "Mickey Mouse." Carnegie's ideal for speechmaking was perceived to be sparkle and spunk more than substance and solid substantiation.

Dale Carnegie Associates Inc.

The international demand for Dale Carnegie instruction, however, grew exponentially. In 1912 Carnegie offered speech instruction in YMCAs. He discovered that if persons spoke on something or someone that angered them they became so immersed in their comments that they soon gained great confidence and their fears and stage fright disappeared. The success of Carnegie's pedagogic approaches resulted in increased self-worth and acceptance. In 1954, the Carnegie programs were incorporated as Dale Carnegie Associates, Inc., and established in Europe, Australia, Asia, and South America. I knew a man in Cologne, Germany, who held the Carnegie franchise for a large region of Germany. He, and those he employed, earned a substantial income. At present over 2,700 professionals deliver Dale Carnegie courses in 85 countries and in 30 languages. At least eight million persons around the globe are graduates of Dale Carnegie courses.

Best Selling Book

Dale Carnegie also achieved a high profile for his best-selling book, *How to Win Friends and Influence People*. The book was first published in 1936, and since then, over 15 million copies have been sold. The Library of Congress designated Carnegie's work the seventh most influential book of all times. Among prominent persons who profess admiration for Carnegie offerings is Warren Buffett of Omaha, Nebraska. Buffett took the Dale Carnegie Course as a twenty-year-old and exhibits the Carnegie diploma in his office.

The table of contents for *How to Win Friends and Influence People*, is:

1. Fundamental techniques in handling people

2. Six ways to make people like you

3. Twelve ways to win people to your way of thinking

4. Nine ways to change people without giving offense or arousing resentment

5. Letters that produced miraculous results

6. Seven rules for making your home life happier

A Missouri Beginning

Dale Carnagey was born in 1888 in Bedison near Maryville, in far northwest Missouri. He attended the one-room schools nearby. As Dale approached notoriety, he found that his name was often misspelled. He changed the spelling to Carnegie, the same as the legendary Andrew Carnegie, and eliminated the confusion. Dale grew up on a farm outside of the city. He relished speaking roles and participated in a high school debate competition in Marysville and Warrensburg. When he was sixteen, his family moved to another farm near Warrensburg, Missouri, where Missouri State Normal College was located (now the University of Central Missouri). Carnegie was not an eminent student, but was ambitious and cherished the fact that he spoke with greater vigor and enthusiasm than most of his peers. He joined the debate squad but was not overly successful. His fellow students perceived him as an impoverished boy from the farm who wore outdated clothing.

A change came about when Dale attended a Chautauqua lecture in Warrensburg. He was impressed by the speaker's techniques and emulated his style of speaking with great success. After a time, Carnegie attracted notoriety on campus and in turn was sought out by his fellow students to offer them speech instructions. Carnegie took a required Latin course, failed, and left the college in 1908 without completing his bachelor's degree. He took a sales position, first selling correspondence courses to farmers, then meat products for the Armour Packing Company in the Omaha region. He became the top salesman in the company. Carnegie resigned from Armour in order to attend the American Academy of Dramatic Arts in New York. He tried acting, but concluded that his skills were best directed toward teaching public speaking in YMCA classes. The classes were so successful that he soon launched classes at YMCAs in other cities. He co-published a book on *The Art of Public Speaking* and the following year spoke to an overflowing crowd at Carnegie Hall.

Advice for Speakers

After serving in World War I, Carnegie visited the famous Speakers Corner in the northeast section of Hyde Park in London. My wife and I visited the Corner a few times when we lived in London where I taught at Pepperdine University's Study Abroad Program in 1990. Carnegie observed that the speakers who attracted the largest audiences were the most enthusiastic. He therefore centered upon enthusiasm as a primary characteristic of successful speaking.

To obtain some sense of Carnegie's insights, considers these two quotes:

> "You can make more friends in two months by becoming interested in other people than you can in two years by trying to get other people interested in you."
> — Dale Carnegie, *How to Win Friends and Influence People*

> "Personally I am very fond of strawberries and cream, but I have found that for some strange reason, fish prefer worms. So when I went fishing, I didn't think about what I wanted. I thought about what they wanted. I didn't bait the hook with strawberries and cream. Rather, I dangled a worm or grasshopper in front of the fish and said: 'Wouldn't you like to have that?'

Why not use the same common sense when fishing for people?"
— Dale Carnegie, *How to Win Friends and Influence People*

Personal Life

Dale Carnegie was married twice. He met Lolita Baucaire in Europe in 1921 and they married. They divorced ten years later in 1931. Carnegie married Dorothy Vanderpool, his former secretary, in Tulsa, Oklahoma, in 1944. Dorothy had two daughters by a previous marriage and Dale and Dorothy gave birth to Donna Dale Carnegie.

In 1955 Central Missouri State University conferred an honorary doctorate upon Dale Carnegie. In 2006 a bust of Carnegie was placed in the Hall of Famous Missourians in the Missouri State Capitol at Jefferson City. Dale Carnegie died of Hodgkin's disease and kidney failure November 1, 1955, in Forest Hills, New York. He is buried in the Belton, Missouri, Cemetery, beside his daughter and parents, his grave marked by a nondescript stone.

7
George Washington Carver (1864-1943): Missouri Agricultural Scientist

I was already a reader when I entered the first grade because of my schoolteacher mother. I looked forward to "My Weekly Reader" published by the American Education Press of Columbus, Ohio, specifically for elementary school students. We paid for our own, and I recall bringing the money to school—twenty cents a semester. I especially loved to read about inventions and scientific breakthroughs. For some reason, a report on George Washington Carver and his experiments with the uses of peanuts captured my imagination in the first

grade in 1935 and 1936. I knew about peanuts because we grew our own and roasted them on top of our wood stove in a ten by fourteen aluminum pan. I was captivated by what Carver developed from this delectable ground nut. At that time I only connected Carver with Tuskegee Institute in Tuskegee, Alabama, and didn't know of his Missouri years.

Missouri Upbringing

George Washington Carver was born, likely in 1864, as a slave in Diamond, near Joplin, Missouri. His mother, Mary, was purchased in 1855 by Moses Carver, a White farmer who had reservations about slavery but needed farm help. Soon after his birth, George's mother, sister, and George were kidnapped from the Diamond farm and sold in Kentucky. Moses Carver hired a neighbor to locate the three, but the neighbor only managed to bring George back to Missouri by trading one of Moses' finest horses for him. Carver knew little about his mother and father. He was raised by Moses and his wife, Susan Carver.

Since George was frail and sickly, Susan taught him how to cook, mend, embroider, and take care of the laundry. George was especially interested in gardening and not only loved working with plants, but learned from Susan how to prepare simple herbal medicines. Having an inquisitive mind, George learned how to preserve the best seed and to utilize fertilizers and soil conditioners. He also experimented with natural pesticides and fungicides. In the neighborhood, he was nicknamed "The Plant Doctor" and was consulted by local farmers regarding their gardens, fields, and orchards.

In 1875, at age 11, George left the Carver farm to attend an all-Black school in Neosho, Missouri. A childless African-American couple, Andrew and Mariah Watkins, took George in, and he helped them with household and gardening choirs. Mariah was a midwife and nurse, and George acquired additional insight into medicinal herbs. She also impressed upon George her devout faith. After two years George despaired over the quality of education he received and moved to Kansas. For the rest of the 1870s, George moved to various Midwestern towns pursuing education and living by the skills he learned from his foster mothers. He graduated from Minneapolis High School in Minneapolis, Kansas, 110 miles north of Wichita. He next applied to Highland College, was accepted, but when he arrived was turned away because he was an African-American. Highland was found in 1858 and located 30 miles west of St. Joseph, Missouri.

College Years

George was approaching the middle twenties when in Winterset, Iowa, southwest of Des Moines, he assisted a white family named Milholland. They encouraged him to enter Simpson College, a Methodist school in Indianola thirty miles east. He studied music and the arts anticipating teaching in high school. One of his teachers, Etta Budd, wondered if he could make much of a living in the areas of his studies and upon learning of his skills with trees, plants and flowers encouraged him to apply at Iowa State University, Ames, north of Des Moines to study botany. The outcome was that George Washington Carver became the first African American to earn a Bachelor of Science degree at Iowa State.

Carver's professors were impressed with his investigations of fungal infections in soybeans, and they asked him to stay on and pursue a Master of Science degree. He pursued studies under the tutelage of L. H. Pammel, a noted mycologist (fungal scientist), who did research at the Iowa State Experimental Station. With a master's in hand in agriculture,

Carver received offers for a position in plant diseases. The one that attracted him the most was a post at Tuskegee Institute where the heralded Booker T. Washington was president.

Booker T. Washington (1856-1915) was born as a slave in Virginia. When his mother was freed in 1865, she moved to West Virginia to be with her husband. Upon finishing high school, Booker attended Hampton University, a traditional Black school in Hampton, Virginia, near Virginia Beach. He pursued additional education at Wayland Seminary, now Virginia Union University in Richmond, Virginia. In 1881, Washington was recommended to found Tuskegee Institute in Tuskegee, Alabama, between Montgomery and Auburn. By the 1890s Washington became one of the most important African-America leaders in the United States. The Tuskegee Institute

Booker T. Washington.

prospered because of wealthy white supporters including Julius Rosewald, John D. Rockefeller, Andrew Carnegie, George Eastman, and Theodore Roosevelt. With money available, Washington prevailed upon George Washington Carver to move to Tuskegee and establish a school of agriculture.

Tuskegee Institute

Carver proceeded under various obstacles but soon gained great respect from the area farmers. He persuaded them to feed their hogs acorns, and to spread swamp muck on their fields instead of fertilizers. A significant recommendation of his was crop rotation; one year planting cotton in a field, and the next year peanuts, soybeans and sweet potatoes. Farmers relished the increased cotton yield, but as yet there was not a market demand for peanuts. Though Carver worked with other plants, his major success was with peanuts and he became known as the "peanut man." He developed more than 300 products from peanuts including milk, cooking oils, paper, cosmetics, soaps, and wood stains. He even experimented with peanut-based medicines such as laxatives, antiseptics, and goiter reduction.

Later Life

In his later years, Carver was widely recognized for his expertise as the stories in *My Weekly Reader* indicate. He traveled throughout the south to promote racial harmony. He was even invited by Mahatma Gandhi so as to consult on nutrition and farming practices in India. He became a special friend of Henry Ford.

A George Washington Monument stands in Diamond, Missouri, on the farm where Carver was born, the first created for an African-American. He was posthumously inducted into the National Inventors Hall of Fame. A museum stands on the campus of Tuskegee University in honor of Missouri-born George Washington Carver.

Photograph by Jessamyn. Copyright Creative Commons.

8
Winston Churchill (1871-1947): The Missouri Winston Churchill, Novelist

Many Missourians are aware that Winston Churchill (1874-1965), the famous World War II British Prime Minister, cast Missouri into global limelight through making a major address at Westminster College in Fulton, Missouri. The date was March 5, 1946, and in his speech Churchill popularized the phrase, "the Iron Curtain," alerting even President Harry Truman, who was present, to the realization that a cold war with Russia was inevitable.

Now late in the second decade of the twenty-first century, few are aware that Missouri had its own internationally acclaimed Winston Churchill (1871-1947) almost a half-century before the notorious Britisher's Missouri address.

The Birth of a Novelist

Winston Churchill was a novelist, born in St. Louis. It is impressive that the number one best-selling novel in the United States every other year, beginning in 1898 and for the next decade, was written by St. Louis-born Winston Churchill. He published seven substantial best-selling novels starting in 1898 and stopped publishing novels in 1915. His novel *Richard Carvel* sold almost a million copies. St. Louis was the setting for *The Crisis*, another highly successful book. All his best sellers were historical novels. Churchill left Missouri in 1899 when he was twenty-eight and moved to New Hampshire, where he lived until his death.

I heard of the novelist before knowing anything about the British Prime Minister who came to that office in 1940. My mother was an inveterate reader. She was a graduate of Southwest Missouri State Teachers College in Springfield, Missouri in 1924 (now Missouri State). She taught high school in Bates County, south of Kansas City, and Thomasville in

Oregon County, east of West Plains. By the middle 1930s, she had four children and spent full time raising them. But she read. The library in Thayer, Missouri, where we lived, permitted each person with a library card to check out three books a week. In the late 1930s, we walked a mile to the library once a week to return our books and check out new ones.

Along with other novels, my mother read those of Winston Churchill. I read Mark Twain, the Rover Boys, and Mark Tidd books. I don't know when I first read Winston Churchill, but I do recall reading at least two novels while at an Alton, Missouri high school in the early 1940s. My favorite was *The Crisis*, set in St. Louis before and during the Civil War. I especially loved historical novels.

Churchill's Education

Churchill was educated at Smith Academy, a boy's school in St. Louis founded by William Greenfield Eliot in 1854. Eliot was also the founder and chancellor of Washington University, and was the grandfather of the celebrated poet T. S. Eliot (1888-1965), who was born in St. Louis and also attended Smith Academy. After various changes and mergers over the years, the school is now the Mary Institute and Saint Louis County Day School in Ladue, a St. Louis suburb.

After graduating from Smith, Churchill enrolled in the Naval Academy at Annapolis, Maryland, graduating in 1894. He entered the Navy and became editor of the Army and Navy Journal. After mustering out, he accepted a position as managing editor of Cosmopolitan Magazine. Having independent wealth, he left the magazine to spend full time writing novels. He not only published twelve novels but was also a poet and essayist.

In 1895, Churchill married Mabel Harlakenden Hall. The New England background of his forebears appealed to Churchill, and in 1899 he built a house in Cornish, New Hampshire, designed by Charles Platt of the Cornish Art Colony headed by Augustus Saint-Gaudens. Cornish is south of Hanover where Dartmouth is located, on the Connecticut River. He was elected to the state legislature in 1902 and 1905, and in 1912 ran for Governor and lost. He toured World War I battlefields and produced a book on his observations, but that ended his literary efforts except for a book in 1940 in which he set forth his religious views. The Prime Minister, aware of the Missourian's prior claim to fame, used the name Winston Spencer Churchill on his publications.

Even at fourteen, I was something of a romantic. I adored *The Crisis* because the underlying plot gradually recounted Stephen Brice's mesmerization with Virginia Carvel, a highly attractive woman. Because of family upbringing and opposing views over slavery, they were deeply conflicted over entering into a relationship throughout most of the novel. Stephen grew up in Boston among "Puritan" abolitionists, and Virginia came from a well-to-do Maryland slave-owning family. They first met at a slave auction in St. Louis at which Stephen outbid Virginia's representative for a slave she wanted for her personal attendant, and Stephen wanted in order to give her freedom. Even though Virginia was very upset at having lost, she felt a spark of fascination for her opposing bidder. This smoldering attraction supplied an alluring undercurrent throughout the book. Churchill effectively pursued their confliction in climactic fashion until late in the novel.

Stephen's proposal of marriage came in Abraham Lincoln's office after the President agreed to pardon Virginia's cousin for spying.

> Then, overcome by the incense of her presence, he
> [Stephen] drew her
> [Virginia] to him until her heart beat against his own. She did not
> resist but lifted her face to him, and he kissed her.
>   "You love me, Virginia!" he cried.
>   "Yes, Stephen," she answered, low, more wonderful in her surrender than ever before. "Yes—
> dear." Then she hid her face against his blue coat. "I—I
> cannot help it. Oh, Stephen, how I have struggled against it! Ho
> w I have tried to
> hate you, and couldn't. No, I couldn't. I tried to insult you, I did i
> nsult you. And
> when I saw how splendidly you bore it, I used to cry."
>   "Virginia, will you marry me?"
>   "Yes."[1]

---

[1] Winston Churchill, The Crisis (New York: McMillan, 1901), p. 514.

Lincoln, in his dying days, reconciled both Stephen and Virginia and the North and the South.

Not only does *The Crisis* depict a titillating love affair but it contains an apt depiction of St. Louis in antebellum and Civil War days. Churchill frequently interjected historical figures. In the "Afterword" he wrote:

> "The author has chosen St. Louis for the principal scene of this
> story for many reasons. Grant and Sherman were living there
> before the Civil War, and Abraham Lincoln was an unknown
> lawyer in the neighboring state of Illinois."[2]

In 1902 the novel was adapted into a play and produced on Broadway. William N. Selig produced *The Crisis* as a silent historically dramatized movie in 1916.

The Missouri Winston Churchill died of a heart attack in Winter Park, Florida, in 1947.

---

[2] p. 521.

9

Champ Clark (1850-1921): Almost President Missourian

Missouri's favorite son, Speaker of the House and Democrat Champ Clark, in June 1912 stood an excellent chance of becoming the next President of the United States. The Republican vote in 1912 was divided between William Howard Taft and Theodore Roosevelt in such a way that whoever was on the Democratic ticket was destined to win the election. Theodore "Teddie" Roosevelt was president from 1901 to 1909. Republican William Howard Taft was his successor from 1909 to 1913. Roosevelt decided to run again in 1912, but regardless of Roosevelt's popularity, Taft was selected at the Republican National Convention in Chicago in June. This was the first year

Champ Clark as U.S. Speaker of the House of Representatives. c. 1915.

for Republican presidential primaries, and in the twelve states that held elections, Roosevelt won 278 votes compared with Taft's 48, even winning in Taft's home state of Ohio. The convention, however, selected Taft. Backers of Roosevelt encouraged him to run as a Progressive "Bull Moose" Party candidate. In the November election, he received more votes than Taft, but both lost to Democratic Governor of New Jersey, Woodrow Wilson.

The Democratic National Party Convention was held in Baltimore from June 25 to July 2. The Democratic Primary elections clearly favored House Speaker Champ Clark of Missouri. So confident was Clark of winning that he decided against attending the convention, a not unusual course of action at that time. On the first ballot, Clark received 440½ votes to 324 for Governor Wilson. By the ninth ballot, Clark clearly received more votes than all the other candidates. The rule of the Convention, however, demanded a 2/3 majority. Still, the expectation was that Clark would eventually win, and at one point Wilson was on the verge of sending a concession speech to the Convention. On the ninth ballot, Tammy Hall, the New York City Political Machine threw its support behind Clark. At that point, William Jennings Bryan, formerly a three-time popular presidential candidate of the Democratic Party, opposed Clark on the grounds that Clark was a tool of Wall Street. Bryan had consistently posed as "The Great Commoner" favoring western traders and farmers over moneyed north-easterners. It was suspected that Bryan hoped to obtain the candidacy for himself. By the 30th ballot, Wilson started to move ahead and finally received the necessary votes on the 46th ballot. Clark came that close to being elected President of the United States because Taft and Roosevelt split the Republican vote in the November 1912 election. It would have been interesting to see what Clark would have done had he achieved the presidency in 1912, and if re-elected four years later in 1916, since he objected to entering World War I and the establishment of a national draft.

The Move to Missouri

James Beauchamp "Champ" Clark was born near Lawrenceburg, Kentucky, west of Lexington. His father was a jack-of-all-trades including teaching, dentistry, and wagon making. Champ's mother died when he was three. His father hired him out to a farmer whom Champ later admired as a model of work and learning. Champ attended school, was an apt student, and read as much as he could, including William Wirt's *Life of Patrick Henry* that caused the young reader to aspire to be a lawyer and congressman.

At seventeen, Clark enrolled at Kentucky University (now Transylvania University) in Lexington. Kentucky University was a private University administered by Disciples of Christ leaders. Disciples of Christ members were sometimes called Campbellites because their prominent polemicist was Alexander Campbell of Bethany, West Virginia. To continue his education, Champ taught school in the summers. After two years at Kentucky, Clark was expelled from the University because he shot a student in self-defense in the heat of an argument. Later Champ was invited to re-enroll, but he decided instead to attend Bethany College which Alexander Campbell founded in 1840. Clark graduated in 1873 as first in his class. He was highly regarded both for his academic capabilities and his commitment to leadership among the Disciples.

Lawyer, Politician

Shortly after graduating from Bethany, Clark, at the recommendation of a Bethany teacher, was appointed president of Marshall College in Huntington, West Virginia. He was twenty-three and the youngest college president in the United States. While serving as president,

The Champ Clark Bridge over the Mississippi River at Louisiana, Missouri. Photo by Mdcastle.

Champ traveled down the Ohio River to Cincinnati, Ohio, where he pursued a law degree at the Cincinnati School of Law. He graduated at the top of his class, and thinking that Kansas offered a great opportunity in law and politics moved there. Unable to find a position his next move determined his future. He heard of a position as Superintendent of Schools in Louisiana, Missouri, north of St. Louis, on the Mississippi River. A year later he left the school and began practicing law. In 1877, age 27, he ran for city attorney and was elected. He ran for the Missouri State Legislature in 1878 but failed. In 1880 he was elected city attorney in nearby Bowling Green. He resigned that post to run for Assistant Prosecuting Attorney for Pike County, and then won the Pike County prosecuting attorney post.

All the while, Champ Clark was active as a Christian Church (Disciples) member. When he taught west of Lexington in Anderson County, Kentucky, he organized the Christian Church Sunday School. According to his biographer, W. L. Webb (1912),

> He was the superintendent of the Sunday-school and it was the most successful one that the church had ever had…He organized the Sunday-school into a body of coherent and enthusiastic workers. Teachers and pupils found a new zeal, the attendance became large. Mr. Clark systematized the study of the Bible for his classes and taught the use of concordances and

other Biblical works…The whole community felt a new fascination for Sunday School work and the interest became tense.[1]

In December 1881, at age 31, Champ Clark married Genevieve Davis Bennett from a notable Missouri family in Auxvasse, Missouri, northeast of Columbia. The Clarks had four children, but Champ Clark, Jr. and Anne Hamilton Clark died in infancy. The two older ones survived into adulthood, Joel Bennett Clark (who changed his name to Bennett Champ Clark) and Genevieve Champ Clark. Bennett was a Missouri Senator from 1933 to 1945 and later a Federal Judge. Champ's wife, Genevieve was born near New Bloomfield in Callaway County, Missouri, just northeast of Jefferson City. Her parents were of British stock and substantial landowners in Callaway County. She attended the University of Missouri, the first year the University enrolled female students in 1869. Mrs. Clark pursued a lifetime of reading, and the family possessed a large library.

Missouri Politics

Campaign button. 1912. Lucke, Badge & Buttons.

Champ Clark entered Missouri politics in a major way in 1888 by being voted into the State Legislature. In 1892, he was elected to the United States House of Representatives but failed to win again in 1894. Not to be deterred, he was re-elected in 1896 and served the next twelve terms (twenty-four years) until 1921. During these years Champ Clark served as speaker of the House in 1911. He supported agricultural interests over those of industry. He supported women's voting rights, income tax, and the direct election of United States Senate. When Woodrow Wilson became president in 1913, Champ Clark helped push Wilson's "New Freedom" progressive legislation through Congress. In 1920, people tired of Wilson's progressivism and voted for a Republican majority, and Champ Clark lost his Speaker's role.

Champ Clark died on March 2, 1921, and is buried in the Bowling Green, Missouri, City Cemetery. He has been the only Missourian to serve as Speaker of the United States House of Representatives, serving

---

[1] William L. Webb, Champ Clark (New York: Neale Publishing Company, 1912), p. 34.

six years and 357 days. Clark aspired to be President of the United States, and it seemed within his grasp. But it didn't happen. The words of the once popular poet John Greenleaf Whittier seem appropriate.

"For all sad words of tongue and pen, The saddest are these, 'It might have been.'"

—John Greenleaf Whittier

10

William H. Danforth (1870-1955): The Checkerboard Philanthropist

Checker Board Square is located near the Mississippi just south of I 64 in St. Louis. The Checker Board is the logo of Purina Mills and was created in 1904 for livestock feeds. Through the years the logo was printed on boxes of whole wheat Ralston breakfast food, for some of us a favorite, and later on boxes of wheat, corn, and rice chex, which we made into a baked worcestershired party mix, especially at Christmas time.

The Ralston-Purina Company was founded by William H. Danforth who commenced mixing feeds for farm animals in 1894. The Danforth Foundation, founded by William H. Danforth in 1927, finally closed in 2011. Over the course of that time the Foundation gave grants totaling

more than 1.2 billion dollars (perhaps 10 billion in 2018) much of it to projects in St. Louis and to Washington and St. Louis Universities. The last seventy million dollars was given to the St. Louis Donald Danforth Plant Science Center.

Born in Missouri

William H. Danforth was born in Bird's Point, Mississippi County, Missouri, just west of Cairo, Illinois. As a sickly child, he was dared by a teacher to be the "healthiest boy in class." He accepted the challenge and pursued a life's goal that served him well in his own health, business acumen, and remarkable philanthropy. Later in his famous book *I Dare You* (1931), he wrote: "I dare you, boys and girls, to make life obey you, not you it. It is only a shallow dare to do the foolish things. I dare you to do the uplifting, courageous things." Life should be, he contended, a perfectly proportioned balance of the physical, mental, social, and religious. He drew a square and placed one of the four words on each side of the square.

Danforth commenced his college education at Berea College thirty-five miles south of Lexington, Kentucky. His attendance at Berea cast a long shadow on his future. He became a supporter of the college, a board member and at the time of his death in 1955 was chairman of the board.

Danforth Chapel, Berea College.

He especially befriended William J. Hutchens, president of Berea from 1920 to 1939. Hutchens was the father of Robert Maynard Hutchins who served as president of the University of Chicago from 1929 to 1945 and attracted national attention because of his unique outlooks on education. Berea was a notable college because, when it opened in 1855, women and African-Americans, and especially students from Appalachia, were admitted. Berea took a work-study approach and at no time in its history did students pay tuition. Danforth from his Foundation, founded in 1927, built a chapel at Berea in 1938, one of twenty-four built on college campuses and elsewhere.

To complete his degree, Danforth entered Washington University and graduated in 1892. At first, he tried brick-making, but soon turned to feed mixing because of the steady market demand. Ralston-Purina Mills later manufactured feeds not only for farm animals, but also household pets, giving the name chow to each type, such as dog chow. The business proved quite successful especially during World War I. In 1894 Danforth married Adda Bush, and to them were born Dorothy (Mrs. Danforth Compton) and Donald, the latter who succeeded William H. as chairman of the board of Purina Mills.

World War I and Later

During the First World War, Danforth, though 47, served in the Third Division of the American Expeditionary Forces. He became the general YMCA secretary for the division, establishing canteens and recreation centers across Europe. He also organized athletic events and religious services.

In 1924, Danforth with a group of friends organized the American Youth Foundation to teach young men and women Christian ideals. As president of the Foundation, Danforth helped establish Camp Miniwanca on Lake Michigan near Shelby, Michigan. He spent the next thirty summers at Camp Miniwanca inspiring and counseling the campers. Danforth built a chapel at the camp, completed in 1941.

The Danforth Associates

William H. Danforth was especially interested in education and religion. The Foundation funded several programs dedicated to these goals. The Danforth Associates Program was launched in 1941 to improve teaching and learning on universities campuses and to promote teacher-student discussions of religion. From as early as I can remember, I heard radio jingles for Purina Mills feed on KWTO, Springfield. In 1955 we moved to Dubuque, Iowa, where I was a professor of communication at the University of Dubuque. The dean, Leo Nussbaum, asked me if Dorothy and I would serve as Danforth Associates on campus. That was the first time we had heard of Danforth, but we were soon to learn much more. We attended a week-long Associates program in August 1956 at Miniwanca, the camp of the American Boy's Club in Shelby, Michigan, north of Muskegon on the east shore of Lake Michigan. We soon learned about the Danforth Associates and considerable about William H. Danforth. We received a copy of his book, *I Dare You* and a small silver pendant Danforth commissioned and had minted in France at the end of World War I. On the back of the silver piece was the square with first letters of the four words. Danforth died at 85 in 1955, the year before. We also met William J. Hutchins, who was glowingly introduced because of his influence on Danforth. Hutchins died two years later. We heard lectures on education and theology. Three of the memorable speakers were Joseph Haroutunian of McCormick Theological Seminary, Benjamin Mays, President of Morehouse College, and Peter Bertocci, Professor of Philosophy at Boston University. Professor Bertocci was a proponent of the philosophy Personalism, which holds that a sense of person underlies all of reality.

We were able to select free books at the camp. I recall picking paperbacks by Karl Barth, Paul Tillich, Rudolf Bultmann, and Dietrich Bonhoeffer. We were awarded $50 ($500 now?) to purchase religious books and food money for entertaining students in our home. Should we need more, we could apply for a second $50. We lived on the edge of the campus and it was easy for students to walk to our house for a meal. Afterward we discussed religious topics of various sorts. We had good discussions and formed several great relationships with students. Since there were Associates in colleges across the United States, the Associates were divided into regions, ours the upper Mid-West, made up of professors in Illinois, Iowa, Wisconsin, Michigan, Nebraska, South Dakota, North Dakota. We had regional meetings. I was elected head for our region which meant that we returned to Miniwanca in August 1957. The following spring our speaker for the regional conference was Markus Barth, son of the well-known Karl Barth, who taught New Testament at Dubuque Presbyterian Seminary on our campus. We went for a river cruise on the Mississippi. After four years, we became Senior Associates and though we didn't receive funds we could attend regional meetings. When I taught at Penn State, we attended the regional Danforth Associate meetings at a Mt. Pocono resort. In Texas we attended a meeting at the HEB Foundation Camp in Leakey, Texas.

In reflecting on his life, Danforth stated, "I flatter myself that I like new ventures and new experiences. But when it comes to fundamentals, I believe in finding the right foundations and building on them. I'm a poor changer. For instance, here are some of the fundamentals I have never changed: I have been a church member for over 60 years; married to one wife for over 60 years; a lodge member for over 60 years; a Purina man for over 60 years.

William H. Danforth's descendants continued the grants, and in later years gave multimillion grants to Washington University and Saint Louis University. The divided company now belongs to Land O' Lakes, General Mills, and Nestle. Grandson William H. Danforth, M.D., was Chancellor of Washington University from 1971 to 1995, and another grandson, John C. Danforth, served three terms as a Missouri senator. The legacy of William H. Danforth, checkerboard philanthropist, impacts Missouri and elsewhere until today.

Ralston-Purina logo.

11
Walt Disney (1901-1966): MISSOURI ANIMATOR

In the fall of 1990, Dorothy and I lived in the Pepperdine University House just south of Hyde Park in London. I taught Pepperdine Study Abroad students who were in our London program. We often traveled to other locations in the famous black cabs. When the cab drivers discovered we were from the United States, almost all regaled us with accounts of their family visit to Walt Disney World in Orlando, Florida. Everyone has heard of Mickey and Minnie Mouse and a whole host of animated characters. Most Americans know of Disneyland and Walt Disney World. They also recognize the name Walt Disney

Walt Disney. Publicity photo, 1946.

and envision his Hollywood connections. But few know of Walt's Missouri roots. Disney spent fifteen of his first twenty-five years in Missouri.

Walter Elias Disney was born in Chicago in 1901. Because of financial exigencies, in 1906 the Disneys moved to Marceline, Missouri, on route 36 east of Chillicothe, to a forty-acre farm on Route 5. Walt was five when his family traveled by train from Chicago to Marceline. When Walt

Main Street, Disneyland, Anaheim, California.

returned from California for a visit in 1946 as a "home town boy made good" the Santa Fe train depot stirred cherished memories of his earlier arrival. The depot is now a tribute to Walt as the "Walt Disney Hometown Museum." Disney attended the Park School in Marcelina and found impromptu contentment under a large cottonwood tree he designated as his "Dreaming Tree."

In 1909, the family decided that Kansas City offered better opportunities, and they moved there. Walt and Roy, Walt's brother who WBA's eight years older, ran a paper route for several years to help with the family finances. Walt attended Benton Grammar School. He also started drawing, especially copying cartoons, and secured parts in school plays, in one case cast in the role of Peter Pan. He took special art classes at the Kansas City Art Institute while still in school.

When Walt was sixteen, his father bought stock in a Chicago food company and the family returned to Chicago. Walt finished high school at McKinley High on the west side of Chicago, where he was a cartoonist for the school paper. He took night courses at the Chicago Academy of Fine Arts. Walt didn't linger long in Chicago. In September 1918 he joined the Red Cross as an ambulance driver. He was assigned to France in November, but arrived after the Armistice was signed on November 11, 1918. Another driver with whom he became acquainted was Ray Kroc, the McDonalds entrepreneur. Some of Walt's cartoons were published in the army's *Star and Stripes*.

Walt Disney Hometown Museum, Marcaline, Missouri.

The Return to Missouri

After two years away, Disney returned to Kansas City in October 1919. His first job was as an apprentice artist at the Pesmen-Rubin Commercial Art Studio where he produced advertising commercials. In 1920, Walt formed his own company with artist Ub Iwerks, but the business was short-lived. Disney next worked for the Kansas City Film Ad Company. He produced commercials employing a cutout animation technique. After experimenting at home, he concluded that cel animation was more promising and formed a new company with Fred Harman. Cel animation starts with pictures drawn on transparent cellulose and then photographed with overlays. The method, more sophisticated through computer enrichment, is still employed with such animated shows as *The Simpsons*. Walt's company produced cartoons for the Kansas City Newman Theater based on classical materials such as *Aesop's Fables*. They were called Laugh-O-Grams. The initial success paved the way for later cartoons based on *Alice in Wonderland*, but the company went bankrupt in 1923.

A Move to Hollywood

In 1923, now experienced in film cartoon production, Walt Disney sought larger venues and moved to Hollywood where his brother Roy was convalescing. Their first efforts to market animated cartoons met with little success, but then they contracted to produce six *Alice Comedies* with a Davis family. Walt and Roy formed the Disney Brothers Studio which over time was designated the Walt Disney Company. In 1925 Walt employed Lillian Bounds as an ink artist, and they married in July.

Success in Animation

A major boost to Walt's career came in 1928 with the creation of Mickey Mouse, inspired by Walt's pet mouse. Mickey appeared in a cartoon, "Steamboat Willie" in 1928 and Walt himself provided the voice for Mickey until 1947. It was the first post-produced sound cartoon. In 1935 Walt signed a contract with Columbia Pictures to distribute the Mickey Mouse cartoons, and they were marketed internationally to great acclaim. The Disney organization also produced other films including "The Three Little Pigs" in 1933. It was one of the most successful short animations of all time.

In 1934, Disney took up a new challenge and produced a feature-length cartoon entitled "Snow White and the Seven Dwarfs." It was made in full color and with sound. The film premiered in 1937 and received substantial praise from critics and audiences. I remember not only the film but also the cardboard punch-out book based on scenes from the movie my sister Nedra cherished. The Disney studio produced "Pinocchio" and "Fantasia" in 1938. Neither of these movies, however, created the hoped-for revenue, and Roy and Walt launched a public stock offering for the company in 1940.

During World War II, Disney obtained governmental contracts to produce training films for the military. Secretary of the Treasury Henry Morgenthau, Jr., arranged for Walt to produce Donald Duck cartoons promoting the purchase of War Bonds. Walt also turned out satire cartoons, for example, "Der Fuehrer's Face," which won an academy award. I recall seeing the film at the Thayer Theater, and can still sing the theme song. "Wenn der Fuehrer says 'wie ist der master race,' we heil, heil right in the Fuehrer's face!" 'Bambi" was released in 1942, but didn't achieve anticipated returns. In the 1950s, Walt produced a number of full-length films: "Cinderella," "Treasure Island," "The Story of Robin Hood and his Merrie Men," "Alice in Wonderland," and "Peter Pan."

The Last Years

The Walt Disney Company kept producing films under the watchful eye of Walt until his death, and has continued since, now affiliated with Rupert Murdoch's Twentieth Century Fox movie and TV studios. While Walt was still alive, he received an impressive number of awards and honors. He won 22 Oscars based upon 59 Oscar nominations. These are the most ever won by an individual. He received two Golden Globe Special Achievement Awards, as well as an Emmy Award. A number of his films are included in the Library of Congress's National Film Registry.

Theme Parks

In the fifties, Walt started planning a major theme park. He had the planners visit all the parks in the United States to learn of their favorable features and pitfalls. He himself visited Tivoli Gardens in Copenhagen, Denmark, and was impressed with its cleanliness and wholesome entertainment for the whole family. After various possibilities including Burbank near his studios, Walt decided upon a site in Anaheim, Orange County, in California south of Los Angeles. Construction began in 1954 and Disneyland opened in 1955. The central thoroughfare of the park was named Main Street and patterned after Main Street in Marceline, Missouri.

Ten years later in 1965, Walt announced plans to build "Disney World," now "Walt Disney World" in Orlando, Florida. The park opened in 1971. Additions since have created the most visited amusement park in the world, attracting 52 million visitors a year. The Epcot Center opened in 1982 with features similar to a permanent world's fair in tracking human progress. Walt also discussed building a theme park on the St. Louis Riverfront and received considerable encouragement, but some detractors, and the plan fell through.

Before Walt's death at sixty-five, often sentimental about his Marceline, Missouri, upbringing, envisioned a theme park for his hometown. He commissioned his brother Roy to pursue that dream after his death, but Roy was highly involved in the development of Disney World. Walt, through a clandestine agent, purchased 200 acres near Marceline and held an option on another 500. He drew up plans and obtained the good wishes of the town fathers. They named an Elementary School for Walt. But with no one to push the project to its completion, the plans were dropped not long after Walt Disney World opened.

Walt Disney died soon after his 65th birthday of lung cancer. His ashes are interred at the prestigious Forest Lawn Memorial Park in Glendale, California, north of Los Angeles.

12

Wyatt Earp (1848-1929): Lamar, Missouri, Lawman

Lamar, Missouri, is known far and wide as the birthplace of Harry S. Truman, the thirty-third President of the United States. Truman was born in Lamar in 1884. The house where he was born is a State Historic Site. But Truman's family only lived in Lamar a year after Harry was born, then moved to Harrison, Missouri.

Wyatt Earp at age 21 in 1869.

Another man whose name is perhaps as well-known lived in Lamar, Missouri from 1868 to 1871, but his stint as an officer in Lamar is little known. The lawman was the famous Wyatt Earp (1848-1929). Earp became notorious almost a century after his years in Lamar because of the television series, "The Life and Times of Wyatt Earp" which aired from o . The first major movie of Earp's life, "My Darling Clementine" starring Henry Fonda, Linda Darnell, and Victor Mature was released in 1946. In 1994 Kevin Costner starred in "Wyatt Earp." The Hollywood image of Earp was a highly laundered version of the real-life lawman.

Experience as a Lawman

Earp lived in various cities in the United States, but because of the broadcast media, he was best known as a lawman in Dodge City, Kansas, and Tombstone, Arizona. He was a police officer in Dodge City from 1876 to 1877, spent a year in the Black Hills gold rush from 1877 to 1878, then returned to Dodge as the Assistant Marshal from 1878 to 1879. He was known as both a Marshal and a gambler, and befriended gunmen Bat Masterson and Doc Holliday. In 1879,, he joined his brothers Virgil and Morgan as law officers in Tombstone, Arizona, where massive amounts of silver had been recently discovered. Wyatt became the City Marshal and a Deputy United States Marshal. Doc Holliday followed him there. In Tombstone, Wyatt feuded with a local rancher that led to a gun battle at the O. K. Corral. This gunslinger episode became perhaps the most famous gunfight in American history.

The Young Earp

Wyatt Berry Stapp Earp was born March 19, 1848, in Monmouth, Illinois, about 50 miles straight south of Davenport, Iowa. He grew up in Illinois and Pella, Iowa, southeast of Des Moines. His father served as a law officer as well as his older brothers. He was too young to participate in the Civil War, but kept running away in an effort to join up. His father kept pursuing him and bringing him back home. In 1864, the family moved to San Bernardino, California. Wyatt finally left home at 17 in 1865 and worked for the Union Pacific Railroad, grading track and hauling freight. In the meantime, his family moved to Lamar, Missouri in 1868, where his father served as the constable.

Urilla Sutherland. 1870.

In 1869, Wyatt joined the family in Lamar, a town then of somewhat under a thousand. His father became a Justice of the Peace and turned the job of Constable over to Wyatt. Later that year Wyatt met and dated Urilla Sutherland (1849-1870). She was the daughter of William and Permelia Sutherland, managers of the Exchange Hotel in Lamar, and was born in Lake Zurich, Illinois, a northwest Chicago suburb. They were married January 10, 1870, in Lamar by Nicholas, Wyatt's father.

On August 10, 1870, Wyatt bought a lot on the outskirts of town for $50 and built a house. Urilla soon became pregnant with the Earp's first child, but she became ill with what was likely typhoid fever and died. Wyatt sold the lot and house for $75. He ran for Constable against his half-brother Newton and won. His father, however, lost in a race for justice of the peace.

A major question, according to Joe Davis of the Barton County Historical Society in 2013, concerns the burial place of Usilla? In fact, Davis claims even her death is a mystery, since no reports of it survive. He charges that the contention that she is buried in the Howell Cemetery in Milford, Missouri, northeast of Lamar, is an effort by a relative to promote tourism, even though a gravestone placed by the relative is located there. He thinks it more likely that she is buried in the East Cemetery in Lamar without a visible marker. It may be, however, that the circumstances under which Wyatt left Lamar caused him to want his time there to be little known.

Dorothy and I, along with our four children, visited Lamar, Missouri, for two days in the early 1960s. My brother, Owen D. Olbricht, served as minister of the Lamar Church of Christ from 1958 to 1966. We drove around Lamar and saw the Truman house. I don't recall whether we discussed Wyatt and Urilla Earp. My brother was into fly fishing, so I went with him to Lake Lamar where he cast flies and snagged a few bass as the sun was setting.

A Cloud of Suspicion

Wyatt Earp left Lamar under a cloud of suspicion. Earp was in charge of collecting license fees for Lamar which funded the schools. Under the suspicion that Earp was not turning in the funds, Barton County filed a lawsuit against him on March 10, 1971. If that wasn't enough, a taxpayer, James Cromwell, filed a suit against Earp charging that Earp had failed to report to the town the total amount of the money Cromwell had paid in taxes. The town, because of the back taxes Crowell owed, seized his moving machine and sold it for $38. Crowell claimed that Earp owed him the real value of the machine—$75. Still, on March 28, Earp, Edward Kennedy, and John Shown were charged with stealing two horses in the Oklahoma Territory from William Keys, valued at $100 each. On April 6, the Deputy United States Marshal J. G. Owens arrested Earp for horse theft. James Churchill, a Commissioner, arraigned Earp on April 14 and set bail at $500.

Troubles continued for the three alleged horse thieves. Shown's wife Anna charged that Earp and Kennedy got her husband John Shown drunk and threatened his life in order to compel him to assist in the thievery. On June 5, Edward Kennedy was acquitted, but the case remained against Earp and Shown. Earp did not await the trial. Apparently, he saw the handwriting on the wall because he climbed out of his cell onto the roof of the Lamar jail and skipped town. The next episode in Earp's checkered career found him in Peoria, Illinois, not far from the place of his birth. He was arrested three times throughout a year by law officials around Peoria. The charges related to activities in which he was involved at brothels. He may have been serving as a bouncer and strongman, but the constables apparently perceived him to be a pimp.

Final Days

Wyatt Earp didn't live to see the onset of the Great Depression. He died in Los Angeles, June 13, 1929. The real Wyatt Earp was a mixed bag of legitimacy and criminality. The Hollywood Earp was an impressive validation of manliness and a heroic defender of justice.

13
T. S. Eliot (1888-1965): Missouri Nobel Prize Poet

In 1948, St. Louis-born Thomas Stearns Eliot received a call from Stockholm, Sweden, informing him that he had been awarded the Nobel Prize in Literature. In his address at the Prize presentation, Anders Österling stated, "Mr. Eliot—According to the diploma, the award is made chiefly in appreciation of your remarkable achievements as a pioneer with modern poetry." Eliot is the only Missourian ever to receive the Nobel Prize for Literature, inaugurated in 1901. The first American to win the prize was Sinclair Lewis in 1930. A total of thirteen Americans have been so honored, the last was Bob Dylan in 2016 "[f]or having created new poetic expressions with the great American song tradition."[1]

Eliot in 1934

A Missouri Heritage

T. S. Eliot was born into a rich heritage of Missourians and New Englanders. His grandfather, William Greenfield Eliot, was born in Bedford, Massachusetts and graduated from Harvard Divinity School, Cambridge, Massachusetts in 1834. That same year his grandfather accepted an offer from a newly formed Unitarian Church in St. Louis to become its first minister. Twenty years later, in 1853, Eliot founded Washington University and served as Chancellor. The next year he launched Smith Academy as a boy's school and Mary Institute, a girl's school. T. S. Eliot's father, Henry Ware Eliot, was a successful St. Louis businessman. He was named for Henry Ware, Jr., a well-known Harvard professor at Harvard

---

[1] https://www.nobelprize.org/prizes/literature/2016/press-release/

Divinity School who was appointed in 1830. Ware mentored Ralph Waldo Emerson. T. S. Eliot's father was a cousin of Charles William Eliot, noted President of Harvard University, who occupied that office when T. S. was a Harvard student.

T. S. Eliot, the youngest of seven children, was sickly as a child, having been born with a congenital double hernia. He spent his time reading and writing, including poetry. He attended Smith Academy in St. Louis until he was sixteen. During this period, Eliot was enamored with waterfronts both of the Mississippi and the Atlantic Ocean. His family spent summers at Gloucester, Massachusetts, on the shore northeast of Boston. In order to get ready to enroll at Harvard, Eliot studied at the Milton Academy in Milton, Massachusetts, later the prep school of Robert and Edward Kennedy. T. S. entered Harvard in 1906 at age 18.

Beginnings in Poetry

My New Hampshire friend of thirty years, Donald Hall, a United States Poet Laureat in 2006, recently deceased, interviewed T. S. Eliot in New York, and the interview was published in the *Paris Review* in 1959. Hall asked Eliot, "Do you remember the circumstances under which you began to write poetry in St. Louis when you were a boy?" Eliot responded,

> I began I think about the age of fourteen, under the inspiration of Fitzgerald's *Omar Khayyam*, to write a number of very gloomy and atheistical and despairing quatrains in the same style, which fortunately I suppressed completely—so completely that they don't exist. I never showed them to anybody. The first poem that shows is one who appeared first in the *Smith Academy Record*, and later in the *Harvard Advocate*, which was written as an exercise for my English teacher and was an imitation of Ben Jonson. He thought it very good for a boy of fifteen or sixteen.[2]

Fitzgerald was an English author who translated the poems of the medieval Persian, Omar Khayyam.

At Harvard, Eliot was attracted to Irving Babbitt and George Santayana. Babbitt taught French and comparative literature and was a noted literary critic. He argued that moral concern requires rigorous self-discipline and an acute awareness of the potential for both good and evil in oneself and in others. Santayana, a Harvard philosopher, was especially interested in aesthetics. He contended that the discernment of beauty

---

[2] Donald Hall, *Paris Review*, Spring, Summer, No 1, 1959.

springs from essentially permanent and universal feelings, and that beauty and morality are interlaced. Eliot obtained a B.A. in 1909 and an M.A. in 1910. He was briefly the secretary of the Harvard literary magazine, *The Advocate*. From 1910 to 1911, Eliot spent a year in Paris attending lectures at the Sorbonne. A year later he was back at Harvard working on a doctorate. He associated additionally with the philosophers William James, one of the fathers of Pragmatism, and Josiah Royce, who held that all reality is unified in a single all-encompassing consciousness. Eliot, in addition, was befriended by Bertrand Russell from England, who was at Harvard as a visiting professor. Russell argued that the world consists of one substance which is neither exclusively mental nor physical. Eliot focused on the psychology of consciousness, critiquing the views of the French philosopher Henri Bergson. Bergson opposed the perspectives of F. H. Bradley who held neo-idealist outlooks similar to those of Royce. Though Eliot submitted his dissertation, he never returned to Cambridge to defend it and therefore never received the doctorate.

Eliot traveled to Munich, Germany, in 1914 for the summer, and spent some of the time at Oxford. The looming dark clouds of World War I caused him to leave Germany. He started writing but had little success publishing, since his poetry displayed new directions. Ezra Pound, an American in exile, encouraged Eliot and arranged publishing channels. Pound is feted as a definer and promoter of modernist poetry, not only of Eliot but also Robert Frost.

In 1915, Eliot married Vivian Haigh-Wood, an English dancer. She had a history of mental problems and refused to cross the Atlantic because of the war, so Eliot settled in England for the rest of his life. He obtained British citizenship in 1927. As a result of Eliot's acumen in math and languages, he acquired a position in 1917 at Lloyds Bank in London, which he continued until 1925.

The Waste Land

The poem that brought Eliot international acclaim, and for which he is best remembered, is "The Waste Land." The poem is memorable and modern both in its content and form. In the post-World War I years, many cultural goals, presuppositions, and conventions lost their power with populations in the West. Eliot characterized the 1920s landscape as decimated and deserted. The whole civilization was a wasteland. Many persons of Eliot's generation shared his weariness. Such disillusionment is obvious toward the conclusion of the poem.

What is that sound high in the air
Murmur of maternal lamentation
Who are those hooded hordes swarming
Over endless plains, stumbling in cracked earth
Ringed by the flat horizon only
What is the city over the mountains
Cracks and reforms and bursts in the violet air
Falling towers Jerusalem Athens Alexandria Vienna London
Unreal.

The form of "The Waste Land," much like jazz and the art that came to the forefront at that time, offered a disjointed wasteland. The structure was complex and variegated, much as different instruments moving in and out of the front center in a jazz band, or the disarray of images in Picasso's *Guernica.*

Murder in the Cathedral

Eliot in 1923.

In 1927, Eliot was baptized into the Church of England. At that point, he turned to religious themes and contexts. When I taught at the University of Dubuque in the spring of 1955, I directed a student reading a dramatization of T. S. Eliot's "Murder in the Cathedral" depicting the murder of Thomas Becket at the cathedral in Canterbury, England, published in 1935. We staged the production in the university Victorian chapel which seated three hundred people. The reading was well received. Eliot had produced the play in 1935 at the cathedral in Canterbury, where the actual murder took place in 1170. Dorothy and I visited Canterbury in 1995, and the words of Eliot remained vivid in my memory. Becket was the Archbishop of Canterbury and earlier a friend of Henry the Second, but they became estranged, and Henry pronounced off-handed critical remarks that prompted four Knights to murder Becket in the church. A priest in the drama says, after the murder as the play nears the end:

O father, father, gone from us, lost to us.
How shall we find you, from what far place
Do you look down on us? You now in Heaven,

Who shall now guide us, protect us, direct us?
After what journey through what further dread
Shall we recover your presence? When inherit
Your strength? The Church lies bereft.
Alone, desecrated, desolated, and the heathen shall
build on the ruins.
Their world without God. I see it. I see it...
O father, father, gone from us, lost to us.
How shall we find you, from what far place
Do you look down on us? You now in Heaven,
Who shall now guide us, protect us, direct us?
After what journey through what further dread
Shall we recover your presence? When inherit
Your strength? The Church lies bereft.
Alone, desecrated, desolated, and the heathen shall
build on the ruins.
Their world without God. I see it. I see it...

Last Years

Later in life, many re-
quests came to Eliot for
lectures, editing, cri-
tiques, and appearances.
Reflecting on these re-
quests, Eliot stated, "The
years between 50 and 70
are the hardest. You are
always being asked to do
things, and yet you are
not decrepit enough to
turn them down." Eliot

All Angels Churchyard, East Coker, United Kingdom.

also wrote other plays, the most famous of which is "Old Possums's
Book of Practical Cats" (1939), which was made into the Broadway musical "Cats" and staged between 1982 and 2000. "Cats" played for twen-
ty-one years in London and experienced later Broadway revivals.

T. S. Eliot is buried at St. Michaels and All Angels Churchyard in East
Coker, England, three hours southwest of London, the town from where
his forebears migrated in the seventeenth century.

14

Eugene Field (1850-1895): A St. Louis Children's Poet

St. Louis-born Eugene Field (1850-1895) was my favorite grade school poet. My school-teacher mother loved poetry. She had a collection of children's poetry. She checked out poetry from the Thayer, Missouri, Public Library located in the Old Opera House. She often interrupted her household chores by reciting them. She encouraged her four children to memorize poetry. Doris Hackett, my second-grade teacher at the Thayer Elementary School, also relished poetry. She regularly assigned memorization and presentations. I memorized poems for both my mother and Miss Hackett.

I knew as a second grader that Eugene Field had a St. Louis connection. St. Louis was 200 miles northeast of Thayer, but I didn't visit St. Louis until I was eighteen. Nevertheless, St. Louis loomed large in my imaginary seven-year-old world. Sponsors from that city supported Charles Lindbergh's non-stop flight to Paris. His plane was named "The Spirit of St. Louis." St. Louis was the headquarters for the Brown Shoe Company. The company sponsored tours of Robert Wadlow, the world's tallest man from Alton, Illinois. Our grade school class was released so we could go down to the Thayer business district and observe Robert Wadlow riding around on the bed of a truck. Perhaps more than anything, Sportsmans Park (Busch Stadium) in St. Louis was the home of the St. Louis Cardinals, the team of Dizzy Dean, later Stan Musial, Enos Slaughter, Red Schoendienst and the rest.

Little Boy Blue

My favorite poem of Field's, who was designated "The Poet of Childhood," was "Little Boy Blue" (1888). Some have contended that Field didn't write poems for children, but about them. Though the verses are about a boy's death and patently sentimental, they captivated me as a seven-year-old.

Little Boy Blue

THE little toy dog is covered with dust,
    But sturdy and staunch he stands;
The little toy soldier is red with rust,
    And his musket moulds in his hands.
Time was when the little toy dog was new,
    And the soldier was passing fair;
And that was the time when our Little Boy Blue
    Kissed them and put them there.
"Now don't you go till I come," he said,
    "And don't you make any noise!"
So, toddling off to his trundle bed,
    He dreamt of the pretty toys;
And, as he was dreaming, an angel song
    Awakened our Little Boy Blue—
Oh! the years are many, the years are long,
    But the little toy friends are true!
Ay, faithful to Little Boy Blue they stand,
    Each in the same old place,
Awaiting the touch of a little hand,
    The smile of a little face;
And they wonder, as waiting the long years through
    In the dust of that little chair,
What has become of our Little Boy Blue,
Since he kissed them and put them there.

Eugene Field

Eugene Field was born in St. Louis in 1850. His father, Roswell Field, an attorney, filed the celebrated case for Dred Scott and his wife, St. Louis slaves, with the United States Supreme Court. Eugene's mother died when he was six, and he was sent to live with relatives in Amherst, Massachusetts. He entered Williams College in Western Massachusetts in 1868. The next year he enrolled at Knox College in Galesburg, Illinois. In 1870, he enrolled at the University of Missouri but didn't graduate. He instead spent six months in Europe after the death of his father.

Eugene Field House and Toy Museum, Denver, Colorado. Photo by Jeffrey Beall.

In 1873, Field worked as a journalist for a newspaper in St. Joseph, Missouri, where he met and married Julia Sutherland Comstock. They had eight children. He continued his work as a columnist and editor in St. Joseph and St. Louis from 1876 to 1880, and later in Kansas City. In 1881 he worked as an editor in Denver, then moved to Chicago in 1883 to write a column called "Sharps and Flats."

Field's acclaim accelerated through his writing poetry about children. After publishing poems in newspapers and magazines, he put together his first book *A Little Book of Western Verse* in 1889. He followed this collection with *The Second Book of Verse* in 1892. In 1894, he produced *Love-Songs of Childhood*. He died of heart failure in Chicago in 1895. His house was made into the Field House Museum and was dedicated by Mark Twain.

Field's two best-known poems were "The Duel" and "Wynken, Blynken, and Nod."

The "Duel" depicts a spat between a cat and dog. I had observed scuffles of this sort and found the poem both amusing and unsettling.

The Duel[1]

The gingham dog and the calico cat
Side by side on the table sat;
'T was half-past twelve, and (what do you think!)
Nor one nor t' other had slept a wink!
  The old Dutch clock and the Chinese plate
  Appeared to know as sure as fate
There was going to be a terrible spat.
  (*I wasn't there; I simply state*
  What was told to me by the Chinese plate!)
  The gingham dog went "Bow-wow-wow!"
And the calico cat replied "Mee-ow!"

Original Illustrations by Mary Ellsworth, ©1941 by The Saalfield Publishing Company, Akron OH & New York.

---

[1] This poem is in the public domain.

The air was littered, an hour or so,
With bits of gingham and calico,
    While the old Dutch clock in the chimney-place
    Up with its hands before its face,
For it always dreaded a family row!
        (Now mind: I'm only telling you
        What the old Dutch clock declares is true!)
    The Chinese plate looked very blue,
And wailed, "Oh, dear! what shall we do!"
But the gingham dog and the calico cat
Wallowed this way and tumbled that,
    Employing every tooth and claw
    In the awfullest way you ever saw—
And, oh! how the gingham and calico flew!
        (Don't fancy I exaggerate—
        I got my news from the Chinese plate!)
    Next morning, where the two had sat
They found no trace of dog or cat;
And some folks think unto this day
That burglars stole that pair away!
    But the truth about the cat and pup
    Is this: they ate each other up!
Now what do you really think of that!
        (The old Dutch clock it told me so,
        And that is how I came to know.)

"Wynken, Blynken and Nod" is an imaginative, dream-like poem. It has a distinct rhythm, and is fun to recite. The presenter can invite the listeners to repeat with her the 'chorus', "Wynken, Blynken and Nod."

Wynken, Blynken and Nod[2]

Wynken, Blynken, and Nod one night
Sailed off in a wooden shoe,—
Sailed on a river of crystal light
Into a sea of dew.
"Where are you going, and what do you wish?"
The old moon asked the three.
"We have come to fish for the herring-fish
That live in this beautiful sea;

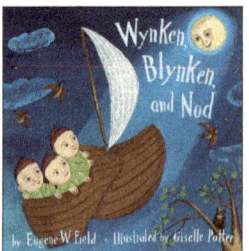

Book cover. Illustration by
Giselle Potter.

---

[2] This poem is in the public domain.

Nets of silver and gold have we,"
Said Wynken,
Blynken,
And Nod.
The old moon laughed and sang a song,
As they rocked in the wooden shoe;
And the wind that sped them all night long
Ruffled the waves of dew;
The little stars were the herring-fish
That lived in the beautiful sea.
"Now cast your nets wherever you wish,—
Never afraid are we!"
So cried the stars to the fishermen three,
Wynken,
Blynken,
And Nod.
All night long their nets they threw
To the stars in the twinkling foam,—
Then down from the skies came the wooden shoe,
Bringing the fishermen home:
'Twas all so pretty a sail, it seemed
As if it could not be;
And some folk thought 'twas a dream they'd dreamed
Of sailing that beautiful sea;
But I shall name you the fishermen three:
Wynken,
Blynken,
And Nod.
Wynken and Blynken are two little eyes,
And Nod is a little head,
And the wooden shoe that sailed the skies
Is a wee one's trundle-bed;
So shut your eyes while Mother sings
Of wonderful sights that be,
And you shall see the beautiful things
As you rock in the misty sea
Where the old shoe rocked the fishermen three:—
Wynken,
Blynken,
And Nod.

Eugene Field was well-respected in his own time for his children's poetry. Several elementary schools were named for him in several different states. Nine of these elementary schools are located in Missouri: Maryville, St. Joseph, Hannibal, Columbia, Mexico, Neosho, Popular Bluff, Springfield, and Webb City.

Courtesy of Eugene Field Elementary School, Poplar Bluff, Missouri.

15
Red Foley (1910-1968): Missouri Ozark Music

In February 1956, the St. Louis Dispatch declared that "Springfield has become the recognized center of the country music world. In fact, it is generally agreed in television, recording, and radio circles, that Springfield, now a city of 90,000, has shaken Nashville, Tennessee, home of The Grand Ole Opry and long-time mecca of hillbilly musicians, to its very foundations." The background for such euphoria was the founding of the famed Ozark Jubilee in 1955 with Red Foley, the premier country musician at that time, as host.

Red Foley, 1944.

Before television, country music achieved major radio listener appeal through Saturday night programs. The first show was the National Barn Dance aired on WWL in Chicago starting in 1924. The program went national on the NBC Network in 1933 and moved to ABC in 1946. The program continued until 1960, when Rock replaced the older music form. The second show was the famous Nashville Grand Ole Opera which officially broadcast on WSM beginning in 1927. The notorious Cincinnati radio station WLW produced the Midwestern Hayride from 1937 to 1972. Somewhat later, the Louisiana Hayride created a major niche on the country western circuits, broadcasting on KWKH, Shreveport from 1948 to 1960. The Hayride was also aired on the CBS Network.

In the almost six years of its existence, the Ozark Jubilee achieved a number of firsts. It was the first network TV program to feature leading country music stars. It was also the first to attract a substantial national audience. Furthermore, Ozark Jubilee holds the record as the longest airing country music series on network television. Red Foley was the key individual in all these attainments.

Red Foley, a redhead, was born in Blue Lick, Kentucky, south of Lexington. He grew up in Berea, where acclaimed Berea College was located.

KWK's Louisiana Hayride Souvenir album cover.

His family encouraged him in music, and by age nine he gave concerts at his father's general store playing piano, banjo, trombone, harmonica, and guitar. After graduating from Berea High School, he served as an usher and gave concerts at a theatre in Covington, Kentucky. Foley enrolled at Georgetown College north of Lexington and was selected by a talent scout to sing with the Cumberland Ridge Runners at the National Barn Dance. In 1933, at 23 Red started recording and became part of Refro Valley Barn Dance show. From that point, his career accelerated rapidly.

In 1939, Foley became the first country western singer to host a network radio show, co-hosted with Red Skelton, on NBC, titled, "Avalon Time." Following "Avalon Time" he spent seven years as a regular on The National Barn Dance. Foley moved to Nashville in 1946, and with the Brown's Ferry Four recorded two Gospel songs "Jesus Hold My Hand," and "I'll Meet You in the Morning," written by the noted Powell, Missouri, songwriter Albert E. Brumley. Also that year he commenced emceeing and performing on "The Prince Albert" segment of the Grand Ole Opry on NBC radio. He continued in this capacity for eight years. In 1950, he recorded what was to become his signature Gospel song, "Just a Closer Walk with Thee," a traditional African-American spiritual that sold three million records. Foley also recorded "Chattanoogie Shoe Shine Boy" that became his trademark. The single was number one on "Billboard's Country Chart" for thirteen weeks and also a hit on the pop chart. Foley also produced "The Red Foley Show" on ABC radio in Springfield, Missouri (1956-1961) sponsored by Dow Chemical.

Publicity photo of Clyde J. "Red" Foley from Ozark Jubilee, ca. 1956

Foley moved to Springfield in the middle 1950s to host Ozark Jubilee on both ABC-TV and radio. The first Ozark Jubilee cast featured Wanda Jackson, Norma Jean, Bobby Lord, Webb Pierce, Marvin Rainwater, Porter Wagoner, and Slim Wilson. Slim Wilson (1910-1990) was a longtime resident of Springfield and constantly in-

Ozark Jubilee cast at the Jewell Theatre, 1956.

volved in country music venues. He was born in Nixa, Missouri, south of Springfield. Nixa has streets named for Ozark Jubilee performers. It has a Slim Wilson Boulevard and a Red Foley Court. Substitute hosts for Foley in 1958, in addition to Slim Wilson, were the acclaimed Eddie Arnold and Jim Reeves. Foley was accredited with discovering Brenda Lee. Lee was born in Atlanta, Georgia, in 1944. Red was in Atlanta with a touring unit of the Ozark Jubilee in 1955 when he was encouraged to put ten-year-old Brenda on the stage. He was so impressed that he invited her to Springfield and she premiered on the program March 31, 1955. She continued to appear throughout the Jubilee's run despite a suit filed by her mother against the show. Ozark Jubilee featured vocals, instrumentals, skits, and square dancers.

Future Years

The anticipated reign of Springfield over country music never happened. In 1957, Brenda Lee and Porter Wagoner left the Jubilee for the Grand Ole Opry. In the early 1960s, Foley was charged with income tax evasion and lost his sponsor. He was later exonerated. In addition, Branson began to weigh in on the music scene.

From 1986 to 1996, I taught at Pepperdine University in Malibu, California. The Dean of Seaver College at Pepperdine, John Wilson, was born in Springfield, Missouri, and at one time as a professor at Missouri State. He was a distant cousin of Slim Wilson. He wrote me about Willa Fae, a high school student who sang duets with him one summer on a KY3 Television show starring Slim Wilson. John wrote:

> Willa Fae and I did not do country music, however. We did what was at that time called "popular" music, which we considered to be much more sophisticated and "classy" than country music.

We shared the dressing rooms at KY3 with many performers connected with the Jubilee. Their show was similar to Your Hit Parade called *Memories*, but John and Willa Fae sang one of the top ten from earlier years, even going back to 1899.[1]

Another frequent singer, more pop than country, was Red Foley's son-in-law, Pat Boone (1934-). Pat married Shirley Foley, Red's daughter in 1953, both age 19. Pat, as well as Shirley, attended Lipscomb Academy in Nashville. Pat's first big hit was Fats Domino's "Ain't that a Shame" in 1955. Pat appeared regularly on the Arthur Godfrey Talent Scout show in New York from 1955 to 1957. Godfrey's scouts brought singers to his attention. Whether the contestants were offered contracts was determined by audience applause. Pat received overwhelming support in several shows and was signed by Godfrey. At the same time, Godfrey decided not to offer a contract to Elvis Presley.

In 2008, I returned from Maine, where we lived in retirement, to Pepperdine University for an internationally attended conference, where I had been a distinguished professor. As a board member for an Institute in St. Petersburg, Russia, I attended our official meeting in a campus conference room. Across from the conference room was a major dining hall at which Pat and Shirley Boone were being honored for a three million dollar gift for the Pepperdine Boone Center for the Family. Pat served a number of years as President of the Pepperdine University Board.

It happened that our meeting ended just as the dinner concluded. While I stood there, the daughter of Red Foley, Shirley Foley Boone, walked out. I stepped over quickly and introduced myself. I told her my sister Nedra Olbricht (later McGill) taught her art at Lipscomb Academy in Nashville. Shirley responded with a smile, "Yes, I remember Miss Olbricht." Shirley walked on, and Pat emerged. I walked toward him and introduced myself. I said to him, "Pat, I shook your hand in front of the newly named Boone Hall at Northeastern Christian College in Villanova, Pennsylvania, in 1961." He searched my face then responded, "We were young then, weren't we?"

Red Foley had a long, impressive career. He was elected to the Country Music Hall of Fame in 1967. His records sold above twenty-five million copies. In September 1968, Foley appeared at two Grand Ole Opry performances in Fort Wayne, Indiana, along with Hank Williams, Jr., son of

---

[1] Personal communication from John Wilson to Thomas H. Olbricht.

Red's long-time friend (then deceased), Hank Williams. On the stage, Red sang with special emotion, "Peace in the Valley." Afterward, he reported to Hank Jr. that he was tired and was going to bed. The singer of acclaim was found dead the next morning. "Peace in the Valley" was sung at his funeral.

An episode of the radio version of Ozark Jubilee in 1954. (Photo Courtesy of Bias/The Library Center.)

16

John Joseph Hogan (1829-1913): A Priest with an Irish Wilderness Dream

Father John Joseph Hogan was born in County Limerick, Ireland, in 1829 and moved to St. Louis in 1847. He studied at the Catholic Seminary in south St. Louis, now known as the Kenrick-Glennon Seminary located in Shrewsbury, Missouri. Father Hogan was ordained as a priest in the St. Louis Archdiocese in 1852. He served in various church positions across Missouri from Potosi to St. Joseph. He had a dream for the thirty thousand Irish refugees who moved to St. Louis because of the 1845 potato blight. They held various positions as domestics, waterfront, rail, and construction laborers. Hogan envisioned that they would  better flourish in a pastoral, sylvan setting, working small acreages and breathing fresh air. He pinpointed an area in northeast Oregon County between the Current and Eleven Point Rivers and drew up plans for a farming community. The region became known as the Irish Wilderness. Complications arose during the Civil War, and gradually the residents moved away. What happened is declared a mystery. The mystery, however, mostly has to do with where the Irish scattered when they left the wilderness, since data is nonexistent.

I frequently heard about the wilderness growing up in Oregon County in the 1930s. The MP-4 camp for the Civilian Conservation Corps, a 1933-42 public works program for unmarried men 17-28, was located to the east of Bardley, Missouri. The Corps worked elsewhere in the region and often traveled in a convoy of troop trucks on the highway past our house. When I went to Alton, Missouri High School a friend or two lived on Hurricane Creek near or in the wilderness. These students rode the bus more than an hour a day to get to school and back. They told of the ruggedness of the country. Raccoon, panthers, bear, and deer roamed the steep forested hills and in the ravines.

Civilian Conservation Corps Camp MP-4, utility building, built 1937. Photo Eric J. Mink, Fredericksburg, VA.

Father Hogan, upon graduating from seminary, was sent as a missionary to the slaves who worked in the lead mines at Potosi and Old Mines southwest of St. Louis in 1852 and 1853. He returned to St. Louis as a priest at Saint John the Apostle and Evangelist Church and then founded Saint Michael's parish. Beginning in 1857 he was involved in a series of missions to transient Irish railroad employees and Catholic settlers located in Chillicothe, Macon City, Brookfield, Mexico, and Cameron, Missouri. In 1859,, Hogan created the Irish Wilderness settlement that continued into the Civil War. Hogan himself, however, relinquished the wilderness for duties at the other missions. In 1868, Father Hogan was appointed Bishop of the new diocese of St. Joseph, which he held until 1893, when he resigned. In 1880 he was also appointed Bishop of the new diocese of Kansas City in which role he continued until his death in 1913.

After much search for land, Hogan purchased almost seventeen thousand acres, or twenty-five square miles, from the Federal Government for twelve and a half dollars per acre mostly in the King township. Several hundred Irish families moved to the settlement. Hogan built a log church completed in 1858. About the church, he wrote: "The quiet solitariness of the wilderness seemed to inspire devotion. Nowhere could the human soul so profoundly worship as in the depths of that leafy forest."

The Civil War wreaked havoc with the community because of the battles, bushwhackers, and guerrillas. A Union Captain burned several structures in the settlement. Hogan asked in anguish who would rebuild the settlement, but the Irish settlers dispersed and it never happened.

As the Civil War wound down in January 1865, a constitutional convention convened in Missouri and included a test oath demanding a pledge of loyalty to the United States. The oath was later declared unconstitutional by the United States Supreme Court. All governmental employees in the state, lawyers, and churchmen were required to subscribe to the oath and were to be arraigned should they refuse. Clergy were given until September 3, 1865, to comply. Father Hogan decided to ignore the requirement. He was indicted in November by Livingston County because of his religious activities in Chillicothe. They charged that,

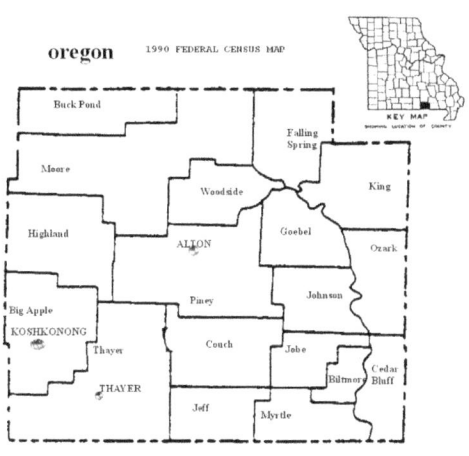

Oregon County, Missouri. 1990 Federal census map.

John Hogan on the third of December, A.D., 1865, at said county, was a priest of a religious persuasion and sect called the Roman Catholic Church, and at the County aforesaid, and on the day and year last aforesaid, the said John Hogan did unlawfully and with force and arms, exercise the function of Priest by preaching to divers persons…John Hogan had not at the time… subscribed and filed the oath of loyalty.[1]

After the arrest Hogan wrote:

---

[1] John Joseph Hogan, *On the Mission in Missouri, 1857-1868* (Kansas City: John A. Heilmann, 1892) p. 124ff.

"...I quickly dressed in full canonicals - Soutane, surplice, stole, birette; and then taking a large crucifix in my right hand, and in my left a large Folio Bible..." "I am a priest; I plead guilty; I confess that I preached the gospel without authority from the State to do so; and if I will have to go to jail for it, you will have to take me there." Bail was paid, and Father was free to go."[2]

Several Protestant ministers left Missouri rather than comply with the oath.

I experienced the Irish Wilderness in the summer of 1946 before my senior year. We had a Future Farmer of America chapter at Alton High School. My uncle, Cleo Taylor, was the vocational agriculture teacher. We skipped summer outings during World War II, but now that the war was over my uncle announced that our chapter would spend two days at Turner's Mill on the Eleven Point River about fifteen miles northeast of Alton. We arrived at the campsite about 5:00 PM in time to build a fire and roast wieners and marshmallows. As it grew dark, we sat around the fire, talking, telling stories and reminiscing about the activities of the 1945-46 school year. The tradition was that no one was permitted to sleep, though those monitoring were self-appointed.

Persons usually tried to sleep on or near the campsite so that the likelihood of getting in a few winks was minimal. Two of my friends and I decided we didn't want to stay up all night, so on the way in we looked for a place to sleep where we wouldn't be disturbed. About a mile from the site we noticed a barn with a hayloft and plenty of hay. We concluded that sleeping on hay would be ideal and the others wouldn't know where

Courtesy Centers for Disease Control and Prevention, US Department of Health and Human Services, Edward J. Wozniak D.V.M., Ph.D.

to find us. Toward midnight we started getting sleepy, so we told our classmates that we needed to wake up, so we were going for a walk. We climbed to the hayloft, but knew enough not to light matches for fear of setting the hay afire. I crawled up a mound of hay looking for a good place to lie down. Almost immediately I felt a significant sting below the nail of my thumb on my left hand. I asked someone to light a match. We didn't see anything in the hay, but my thumb was marked by two

[2] Ibid.

dots of blood, clearly fang marks. We decided that the only thing to do was walk back to the camp and report the bite to Uncle Cleo. By the time we arrived my arm had begun to swell. Uncle Cleo immediately took out his knife, cut slits on the fang marks and began to suck. The standard country procedure then was to suck on the wound under the supposition that the venom would be drawn out. Such was generally believed, but later studies failed to support this remedy. We concluded that the snake was probably a copperhead, of which plenty were around. Our scheme to sleep that night was ruined. We left about 6:30 the next morning so as to be first in line at Dr. Cooper's office.

The Irish Wilderness may be isolated and long neglected, but it surges vividly in my memory. I was eager to learn more about Father John Joseph Hogan, whose actions gave rise to the designation.

17
Scott Joplin (1868-1917): Missouri Ragtime Music

"Missouri, located in the center of America, was the heartland of ragtime."[1]

Sedalia, Missouri, calls itself "The Cradle of Ragtime," and honors Scott Joplin with its "Scott Joplin International Ragtime Festival, founded in 1974.

In the late 1980s, we lived in Malibu, California, where I taught at Pepperdine University. It was not uncommon to see stars in the middle of the day in Malibu. I drove Pacific Coast Highway to pick up a prospective professor at the Los Angeles International Airport. I saw two men standing on the sideway near the highway. All at once it occurred to me that the shorter of the two was none other than superstar Robert Redford.

Portrait of Scott Joplin. First published in St. Louis Globe-Democrat newspaper, June 7, 1903.

I am a fan of Redford, but for more than any other reason, I loved "The Sting," the 1973 movie in which Paul Newman, Robert Shaw, and Redford starred. I liked the plot of the movie, but I loved the music. The music, adapted by Marvin Hamlisch, was ninety percent that of Scott Joplin who achieved acclaim in Sedalia and St. Louis, Missouri. Hamlish (1944-2013) received an Oscar for the musical score of

---

[1] Library of Congress article, "The History of Ragtime."

"The Sting" which featured "The Entertainer." In the middle 1970s, the ice cream trucks blasted out "The Entertainer" to announce their arrival.

Scott Joplin (1868-1917)

At his death, Scott Joplin was designated "the best of the best when it came to writing ragtime music." Scott Joplin was born in the countryside near Texarkana, Texas. When he was still a child, his parents moved into Texarkana. Both of his parents were musically active, his mother Florence singing and playing the banjo and his father Giles the fiddle. Scott showed talent on the piano and took lessons from Julius Weiss, a local German music teacher who introduced him to classical music. Scott left home at the age of sixteen and sometimes traveled alone and sometimes with others, playing the piano, as well as the cornet and violin in bars and dance halls. Joplin experimented with new musical forms that laid the foundations for ragtime. Sometime in the 1880s, Scott settled in Sedalia, Missouri, where he played piano in the bars, clubs, and bordellos. It is thought that he had relatives in Sedalia and attended Lincoln High School, which was African-American according to Edward A. Berlin in his book, *King of Ragtime: Scott Joplin and His Era*.[2]

The culture of Sedalia itself was attractive for African-American musicians. Sedalia was founded in 1860. By the middle of 1890, 14,000 people lived in there. It was at that time the fifth largest city in Missouri. Sedalia was in the region of Missouri where the most antebellum African-American slaves worked on farms. By the 1880s, several Blacks had departed, but several still lived in the northeast section of the city working on railroad crews and as laborers and domestics. The Missouri Pacific and Missouri, Kansas, and Texas railroads entered the city from six directions. Railroaders and travelers frequented the bordellos located above the businesses on West Main Street. The businessmen profited from clientele passing their show windows. The houses of prostitution supported black musicians, and Sedalia became a seedbed for emerging ragtime. Sedalia also attracted summer visitors to the Missouri State Fair held annually from 1901.

In 1893, Joplin organized a band that played in the region near the acclaimed World's Columbian Exhibition in Chicago. When the Exhibition was over, he returned to Sedalia where he took classes at the George R. Smith College for African Americans. Smith College was founded in 1894 and closed in 1925 as the result of a fire that destroyed the main

---

[2] New York: Oxford, 1994.

building. Joplin not only took classes in music, he also started teaching. He reportedly studied classical music, composition, and directing. He was the most astute and tasteful composer of ragtime in the era through incorporating classical modes. He aspired to write for the lyric stage and produced two operas. In all, Joplin composed 44 rags, two operas, and one ragtime ballet. He also co-published seven rags. His most famous composition was the Maple Leaf Rag named for the African-American Maple Leaf Club in Sedalia. By 1914, the sheet music for the Maple Leaf Rag sold one million copies.

Ragtime in St. Louis

Ragtime was mostly piano music early in the twentieth century. The treble notes were played with a "ragged time" or syncopated rhythm, while the bass maintained a metronome-like steady beat. Scott Joplin and others in St. Louis initiated the ragtime craze. Joplin moved to St. Louis in 1901 and remained there until 1907. In St. Louis, he associated with Tom Turpin, Louis Chauvin, Artie Matthews, and music publisher John Stark who moved to St. Louis from Sedalia. The places they frequented were in Chestnut Valley, near the Mississippi River, and roughly on the site of the Scottrade Center. The Scott Joplin House State Historic Site is located at 2658 Delmar Boulevard. Ragtime flourished during the legendary 1904 St. Louis World's Fair, remembered in the celebrated song "Meet Me in St. Louis, Louie." The tune of "St. Louis

Sheet music cover. Shattinger Music Company, 1931.

Blues" was heard in the city as early as 1892 and was related to ragtime. The golden age of Ragtime was the early 1900s. Later revivals occurred in the early 1940s and again in the 1970s ignited by "The Sting."

My Interest

Uncle Cleo Taylor, an early 1930s graduate of now Missouri State University, Springfield, loved popular and church music. He was the Vocational Agriculture Teacher at Alton, Missouri High School. I stayed with him and worked on his farms during my high school years 1943-1947. He constantly sang as we worked and I picked up many of his songs, a number of which were in the ragtime mode. Characteristic was "Hello my Baby," written in 1899 by Joseph E. Howard, with early St. Louis connections, and Ida Emerson:

> Hello my baby
> Hello my honey
> Hello my ragtime gal
> Send me a kiss by wire
> Baby my heart's on fire
> If you refuse me
> Honey, you lose me
> Then you'll be
> Left alone
> Oh baby telephone
> And tell me I'm
> Your own

Other songs were "Alexander's Ragtime Band" (Irving Berlin, 1911), "Five Foot Two, Eyes of Blue" (1914), and "Ain't She Sweet." (Milton Alger and Josh Teller, 1927).

Because of Uncle Cleo's influence, I was attracted to John Philip Sousa band music, Dixie Land Jazz, and Ragtime. In 1959, when we moved to Natick, Massachusetts, we bought an upright piano with a player mechanism. In the nineteen seventies I became enamored with the ragtime music of Scott Joplin. I discovered that two music companies, Aeolian and QRS, sold ragtime rolls, one of Scott Joplin' rags, and a roll of the Maple Leaf Rag a copy of which Joplin himself cut. I also discovered that several 33 vinyl ragtime records were available. I bought a half dozen, played by Joseph Rifkin (Nonesuch Records), Max Morath, who produced a four-part public television program on ragtime, and a recording by the Wolf Trap Ragtime Band. We attended a live concert of the Wolf Trap Band with the famous jazz musician Gunther Schuller conducting at Pepperdine University.

Final Years

Scott Joplin moved to New York in 1911, hoping to promote his ragtime opera "Treemonisha." His health began to fail as the result of syphilis, and his efforts at staging his operas were for the most part unsuccessful.

The end came in 1917. Ragtime slowly waned in Missouri, but its syncopated rhythm still has devotees in Missouri and internationally.

18
Elizabeth Keckley (1818-1907): Missouri Modiste

We live in retirement at the Riverwoods Community in Exeter, New Hampshire. We have an excellent central library and lounges in all four units stocked with books to peruse and take to our apartment. A year ago we picked up a novel by Jennifer Chiaverini, *Mrs. Lincoln's Dressmaker* (2013). The novel tells the story of Elizabeth Keckley,a mulatto dressmaker, and her relationship with First Lady Mary Todd Lincoln, the Lincoln children and the president himself. The novel is well-written and utilizes the available details of that relationship, especially dependent on the autobiography of Elizabeth Keckley, *Behind the Scenes* (1868). Though born in Virginia, Keckley (1818-1907) lived in St Louis from 1847 to 1860 where before returning east she gained freedom from slavery. Her story is amazing.

Early Years

Elizabeth Keckley was born in Dinwiddie, Virginia, south of Petersburg. Her mother Agnes was a domestic slave owned by Armistead and Mary Burwell. Despite the law on educating slaves, Agnes learned to read and write. Elizabeth didn't know who her father was until her mother revealed on her deathbed that he was her white master, Armistead Burwell. Burwell permitted Agnes to marry a black slave of a neighboring plantation, but her husband was forced to move away with his master. Elizabeth started her official duties as a slave at age four and was assigned the responsibility of nursemaid for her mistress's infant. One time she tripped with the cradle and the child scooted to the floor. For this and future missteps the mistress beat her severely.

Mary Todd Lincoln. Photo by Mathew Brady, 1861.

When Elizabeth was 14, in 1832, she was loaned upon his marriage to the Burwell's son Robert. The new wife disparaged Elizabeth and made her life miserable. Robert and his family moved to Hillsborough, NC, where he was a minister and teacher. When Elizabeth was 18, Margaret, the wife, recruited William J. Bingham, a neighbor, to break Elizabeth's pride. Bingham ordered her to undress so he could beat her. When she refused, he tied her hands and feet and proceeded to whip her back until blood gushed out. He whipped her once a week over the next two weeks, but then had a change of heart, and told her that he would beat her no more and asked her forgiveness. Over four years, Elizabeth was forced to have sexual relations with a prominent white man in the community, which she portrayed as bringing about "suffering and deep mortification." In 1839, she had a son by her rapist and named him George after her stepfather. Elizabeth then returned to Virginia where she served Burwell's daughter—Ann Garland and her family. The Garlands had financial exigencies, and Elizabeth took up sewing in order to secure funds for the family.

When the Garlands moved to St. Louis in 1847, they took Elizabeth and her mother along to look after the children and do all the family sewing. In the twelve years that Elizabeth lived in St. Louis she became well acquainted with the large free Black community. She continued to sew for white women in the city. She met James Keckley in St. Louis but rejected his marriage proposal until she could obtain freedom for herself and her son George. It took her two years to persuade her master Garland to free them. In 1852 he agreed to release them for $1200. With the help of Elizabeth Le Bourgeois, her patroness, Keckley secured the necessary funds and was manumitted in November 1855. She stayed in St. Louis and earned enough money to repay her patrons. By 1860, she was able to leave St. Louis and James Keckley, and move with her son George to Baltimore. George enrolled at the newly established Wilberforce University in Xenia, Ohio.

Elizabeth anticipated teaching young Black women her system for cutting and fitting dresses, but that didn't work out, so she moved to Washington, D. C., with the hope that orders in the capital would produce an adequate income. As the deadline approached to acquire a license to live in Washington, lacking the funds, she appealed to her patrons, and a Ms. Ringold persuaded Mayor Berret to give Elizabeth the license free of charge. In a short time, she received sufficient commissions to assure her financial needs. One order came from Mrs. Robert E. Lee, wife of the famous Confederate general, and soon the demands for Elizabeth's talents exceeded her capabilities. A new customer, Margaret McLean of Maryland, made an urgent request for a garment that Elizabeth declined for lack of time. But Mrs. McLean persisted and told Elizabeth that she would introduce her to Mary Todd Lincoln and the president.

Elizabeth met with Mary Todd on the day of Lincoln's first inauguration, March 4, 1861. Mrs. Lincoln invited Elizabeth to the White House to discuss dressmaking. When Elizabeth arrived, she discovered that other dressmakers were there, but as the result of the interview, Mrs. Lincoln chose Elizabeth as her personal modiste. Not only did Elizabeth sew the gowns of Mrs. Lincoln, but she also assisted her in dressing each day.

Elizabeth essentially became part of the Lincoln household, helping with ceremonial and social functions and befriending the children. She was especially involved in comforting the Lincolns upon Willie's death in February 1962. Because of Mrs. Lincoln's desire to wear elegant dresses, Elizabeth was fully occupied designing and assembling an impressive wardrobe and making sure Mrs. Lincoln was fashionably coiffed. During the presidential years, and many after, Elizabeth Keckley was the sole creator of Mrs. Lincoln's wardrobe and her closest confidant.

Quilt made by Elizabetjh Keckley from scraps of dresses for Mary Todd Lincoln. Courtesy Kent State University.

A Care Giver

Elizabeth Keckley was active during the Civil War with an organization for helping Blacks. She launched the Contraband Relief Association in

1862, renamed the Ladies' Freedman and Soldier's Relief Association in 1864. She received funds from several affluent whites, including the Lincolns, as well as prosperous Blacks. The money was employed to provide food, shelter, clothing, and emotional support for slaves recently freed and for wounded and ill soldiers. In her autobiography, Keckley wrote that the former slaves required assistance because in the days ahead, "the road was rugged and full of thorns."

George Keckley, Elizabeth's son, who was more than three-quarters white, enlisted in the Union Army in 1861. He was killed in action on August 10, 1861. Elizabeth received a survivor's pension which today would be $170 a month.

When Abraham Lincoln was assassinated in 1865, Elizabeth Keckley was one of the few persons permitted to assist and console Mary Todd Lincoln. When Mrs. Lincoln moved to Chicago, she insisted that Elizabeth accompany her. After Elizabeth returned to Washington, Elizabeth and Mary Todd corresponded regularly. In 1867 Mrs. Lincoln was deeply in debt. She wrote Elizabeth insisting that she help her in selling items of value including her extensive wardrobe that Elizabeth had crafted. They traveled to New York by train to enlist a broker. Mrs. Lincoln adopted an alias so her impoverishment would not be known. Her efforts to sell the items, however, were soon discovered by the press because of assistance Elizabeth sought from notable persons, and Mrs. Lincoln was widely criticized for trying to dispose of these memorialized objects.

In 1868, Elizabeth Keckley published her autobiography *Behind the Scenes* as an effort to present Mrs. Lincoln in a better light. But her well-intended purpose was largely thwarted by controversy over whether a former slave could write such a book or whether it was appropriate to publicize these personal details about the Lincolns. Others questioned the propriety of a Black employee exposing the private lives of a nationally prominent white family.

In later years, Mary Todd Lincoln cut off all communication with Elizabeth. Because of the controversies surrounding her book and changing dress styles, demands for Elizabeth's skills diminished. In 1892, she was offered headship of the Department of Sewing and Domestic Science Arts at Wilberforce University. The next year she arranged an exhibit of dresses at the Chicago Columbian Exposition. Later in the nineties, she returned to Washington where she lived in the National Home for Destitute Colored Women and Children. She was living in the home when she died in 1907.

Elizabeth Keckley was tormented in slavery and treasured in the Lincoln White House.

19

Sinclair Lewis (1885-1951): Sinclair Lewis in Kansas City

Sinclair Lewis taught a "Sunday School Class" in Kansas City, Missouri, in late 1926 and early 1927. The class was by no means conventional. Those present were churchmen from Protestant, Catholic, and Jewish sanctuaries in Kansas City. He wrote a friend,

Sinclair Lewis in 1914.

> I don't know whether or not I have told you anything about my Sunday School class. I have had from fifteen to twenty preachers coming to lunch with me every Wednesday, and I have had rather remarkable luck in asking them impertinent questions about why they are ministers.[1]

In 1926, Lewis determined to write a book about the foibles, flaws, and perversions of evangelistic ministers. After wrestling with various titles, he settled upon *Elmer Gantry*. Sinclair Lewis as a novelist savored specificity and carefully articulated observations. He concluded that the best way to acquire insight was to initiate conversations with clergymen. Kansas City seemed to him an excellent locality from which to obtain the documentation required. He reportedly stated to a journalist, perhaps tongue in cheek, that he planned to move to Kansas City, but he may have been deadly serious when he declared that Kansas City is "the most typical American city I know."

---

[1] http://paris-of-the-plains.blogspot.com/2016/04/when-sinclair-lewis-got-new-hat.html

First edition cover.

When *Elmer* Gantry appeared in 1927, the book was heralded by many as a frontal attack on American churches. Shortly thereafter, *Elmer Gantry* was banned in Boston, Kansas City, Camden, and a number of other places. But the book was an almost immediate sensation; *Elmer Gantry* was the number one best-selling novel in 1927.

Over the years, "Elmer Gantry" became a common designation for charlatan religious leaders. Thirty years after its debut, the book was mined as a source for a major movie, starring Burt Reynolds, Jean Simmons, Shirley Jones, and Patti Page. Even Boston by that time had no quibbles the showing of the film.

In 1960, my family and I lived in Natick, Massachusetts, fifteen miles from the Boston Hub. Drive-in theatres were the rage. We had four children ages 8, 6, 4, and 2. We owned a 1956 Nash Ambassador that was exceptionally wide and had back seats that folded down. We carried blankets to the car, dressed the kids in pajamas, packed snacks, and traveled west to the drive-in near Shopper's World, the first covered mall in the United States. The older kids watched the cartoons, but one by one they all dropped off to sleep. That was the way we saw *Elmer Gantry*. The movie received many Academy nominations. When the Oscars were announced Burt Lancaster as the Best Actor and Shirley Jones the Best Supporting Actress, I was especially impressed with Shirley Jones. We had seen her in "Oklahoma," "Carousel," and two years later, "Music Man."

Sinclair Lewis

Sinclair Lewis (1885-1951) was born in Sauk Centre, Minnesota, a hundred miles northwest of Minneapolis. Sinclair was studious in his youth and attended Oberlin (Ohio) academy in preparation for taking his degree at Yale in 1908. At Oberlin, he developed an interest in religion which waxed and waned through his teen years. At Yale, he wrote poetry and short stories, and became editor of *The Yale Literary Magazine*. He published his first book in 1912, a Tom Swift-type boy's novel, *Hike and the Aeroplane*. After publishing in several venues Lewis turned out classic novels including *Main Street* (1920), *Babbitt* (1922), *Arrowsmith*, (1925), *Elmer Gantry* (1927), and *Dodsworth* (1929). In the late 1950s, when I taught at the University of Dubuque in Iowa, I read these novels. Since I was located in Sinclair Lewis country, I readily resonated with his style, acumen, and focus.

In 1930, Lewis was momentarily stunned when a Swedish telephone call revealed that he had received the coveted Nobel Prize in Literature. He was the first recipient from the United States to attain that honor. Since 1930, thirteen Americans have received the Prize. One Missourian, T. S. Eliot, born in St. Louis, and his residence until he was twenty-five, was awarded the Nobel for his poetry in 1946. According to the committee, Lewis was voted the award "for his vigorous and graphic art of description and his ability to create, with wit and humor, new types of characters."

The Novel

Elmer Gantry was a hypocritical preacher who inclined more toward seeking booze, women, and greenbacks than converts. Upon graduating from college, Gantry attended a Baptist seminary and obtained Baptist ordination. He was able to cover up several sexual indiscretions but never finished his seminary degree since he was suspended because drunkenness prevented him from showing up for a preaching appointment. For several years he sold farm equipment. After attending an evangelistic crusade of Sharon Falconer, he became so enamored with her ministry and person that he became her manager, lover, and co-evangelist. It is commonly assumed that Lewis modeled Sharon upon the Canadian-born Aimee Semple McPherson. Lewis tried to interview McPherson in Los Angeles without success, but he heard her preach at her Temple.

Gantry, after a time, evangelized on his own, then became the pastor of a large Methodist congregation in Zenith, that is, Kansas City. In early years Elmer attempted to seduce Lulu Baines and much later in Kansas City they revived their clandestine affair. The plot of *Elmer Gantry* is fleshed out by concrete depictions of the beliefs, claims, and practices of the denominations portrayed. Not only did Lewis meet with the clergymen, but he also attended two or three religious services a week the months he was in Kansas City.

While *Elmer Gantry* was a best seller, the book had many detractors. Billy Sunday, a Midwesterner and immensely popular evangelist, designated Lewis "Satan's cohort" and threatened to beat him up. One correspondent invited Lewis to witness a lynching in Virginia—his own.

The Kansas City Sunday School Class

Sinclair Lewis, in his second Kansas City visit, stayed at the Ambassador Hotel in downtown Kansas City, built in 1920. According to the distinguished actress Ethel Barrymore, who was a hotel guest at the same time, Lewis' room,

> …was always crowded with ministers of every denomination whom he was bullying, in the hope, I suppose, of extracting something for his book. He would stride around the room, pointing a finger at one of them after another and saying, "You know you don't believe in God."[2]

1957 Postcard of Ambassador Hotel, Kansas City, Missouri.

The two most important churchmen Lewis visited were William L. "Big Bill" Stidger (1885-1949), pastor of the Linwood Boulevard Methodist Church, and Burris Jenkins (1869-1945), minister of the Linwood Boulevard Christian Church. In his first weeks in Kansas City in late 1926, Lewis stayed with the Stidgers. Stidger was extremely ambitious, always pursuing new avenues of publicity. He designed a lighted revolving cross for church buildings including Linwood. He was one of the first to undertake a major radio ministry; a half million American listeners tuned into his program. He orchestrated the building of a bowling alley on the church grounds. In 1928, he left Kansas City for Boston and taught preaching at the Boston University School of Theology. Sinclair Lewis led Stidger to believe that *Elmer Gantry* would place him in the limelight, but when the book appeared, Stidger was chagrined by how he was depicted.

Burris Jenkins of the Christian Church wasn't as flamboyant as Stidger, but still promoted a non-conventional ministry. Jenkins was born in Kansas and went to Bethany College in West Virginia, founded by Alexander Campbell. He then pursued graduate degrees at Harvard Divinity School. He served as a professor and then president of the University of Indiana, and later as president of Kentucky University. He accepted the Linwood ministry in Kansas City (1907-1945). He went out of his way to attract

---

[2] *From Main Street to Stockholm: Letters of Sinclair Lewis, 1919-1930*, ed. Harrison Smith (New York: Harcourt, Brace, and Company, 1952) 194.

young people by showing movies and holding Sunday Night dances. He developed benevolence programs for the needy of Kansas City. He also launched a radio program and purchased lavish advertising.

Lewis learned much from his Kansas City interviews. However one may assess *Elmer Gantry*— the religionists of Kansas City, Missouri, furnished Lewis detailed documentation. Lewis remarked to a friend, "I got more out of Kansas City for the preacher book than can be imagined."

20
Paul Nagel (1926-2011): Mapping Missouri History

In 1996, I retired from full-time University teaching. I consummated a busy career in teaching and administration and had not published as much as I hoped. Early in the twenty-first century, I was encouraged by my former student, Kathy Pulley, a professor at Missouri State University, Springfield, to publish a book on my Missouri years. The book was much delayed because of other volumes either written or edited, published at the rate of one a year, but finally my Missouri book reached the shelves: Thomas H. Olbricht, *Missouri Memories 1934-1947*.[1]

Photograph by Steven Date. Used by permission.

As I contemplated writing *Missouri Memories* I decided I needed to read a good history of Missouri. After doing a search, I concluded that the book to purchase was, Paul C. Nagel, *Missouri: A Bicentennial History*.[2] I was impressed with the volume, located Nagel's e-mail address, and wrote him. I was pleased to receive an immediate response, and we began corresponding. We developed an immediate rapport and sent attached documents back and forth. In 2006, Dorothy and I along with friends attended a Conference at St. Paul Lutheran Seminary. We arranged to meet Paul and Joan Nagel for a congenial, relaxed lunch near their Minneapolis residence. We discovered that Paul's family had deep Missouri roots and that he and Joan had lived in Columbia from 1969 to 1980 when he was a Vice President at the University of Missouri, and she an archivist at the University Libraries.

---

[1] Thomas H. Olbricht, Introduction by Kathy J. Pulley; Afterword by Brooks Blevins, *Missouri Memories: 1943-1947* (Eugene, Oregon: Wipf and Stock, 2016), p. xi.

[2] New York: Norton, 1977.

Nagel's *History of Missouri* was written in the Bicentennial Year of the United States. About the publication, Nagel wrote: "I am the first to confess that Missouri is difficult to understand…Unfortunately, Missouri reveals little about herself that is not varied, confusing, and contradictory. Her story is as often disillusioning as it is inspiring, for her relationship to the Union has been a mixture of triumph, despair, and embarrassment." Nevertheless, in a more pointed observation, Nagel wrote

For a good reason, Missouri's capital city can remain proud that it is named after Thomas Jefferson, the apostle of limited government and agrarian values. Should the spirit of Samuel Clemens, Harry Truman, and Reinhold Niebuhr—to recall only

a few of the state's more perceptive natives—be among us, they would probably feel right at home.[3]

Paul Nagel (1926-2011)

Paul Nagel was a historian extraordinaire. His specialty was the John Adams family. He published three major works on the family: *Descent from*

---

[3] Ibid, p. xi.

Glory: Four Generations of the John Adams Family (1983); *The Adams Women: Abigail and Louisa Adams, Their Sisters and Daughter* (1987); and *John Quincy Adams: A Public Life, A Private Life* (1997). He published two additional books focused on Missouri: *The German Migration to Missouri: My Family's Story* (2001), and *George Caleb Bingham: Missouri's Painter and Forgotten Politician* (2005). The Adams family descendants named him an honorary member. A book of which he was especially proud: *This Sacred Trust: American Nationality* (1971) he sent to me as a gift.

Early Life

Paul Nagel was born in Independence, Missouri, in 1926. His families were long-time residents of the state having migrated from Germany as early as 1843. They settled in the German region in Warren County and several in Washington, Missouri. Paul's Nagel grandparents moved to Jackson County near Kansas City in 1906. He attended William Chrisman High School on Lexington. His classmates remembered him as sickly and he was held out of school for a year. As he grew older, he became healthier, and was admired for his intellect and debating skills.

Liking to hunt and fish, Paul entered college at the University of Minnesota shortly after World War II. At first, he planned to study mortuary, because he had worked in funeral homes as a high school student. He soon, however, switched to history. He stayed several years at Minnesota earning a B.A., M.A., and Ph.D. He met Joan Peterson, a librarian and they were married in 1948. Joan was an excellent companion and assisted when needed with his research. Regarding the marriage, he wrote, "Joan has proven that if a Minnesota Swede can live with a German Missourian, there may be hope for the 'Show Me' state after all."

Nagel's first major position was as a history professor at the University of Kentucky. Some years passed, and he was appointed dean of the College of Liberal Arts and Sciences. He left Kentucky for his home state and was Vice President for Academic Affairs at the University of Missouri from 1969 to 1980.

Nagel also taught at the University of Georgia and received visiting professorship appointments at Vanderbilt and Amherst. In 1980, he left academia to direct the Virginia Historical Society. The new position permitted him to spend more time writing histories and biographies. In 1992, the Nagels returned to Minneapolis where they lived the remainder of their days.

Paul was working on his last book when I met him. He had a special interest in George Caleb Bingham as an artist and politician because he believed that in both paintings and diplomacy Bingham projected prototypical Missourians.[4] It may be that Nagel's interest in Bingham resulted from a school in the Independence School District being named the George Caleb Bingham Middle School which he possibly attended.

George Caleb Bingham (1811-1879) was born in Virginia. As a result of financial exigencies, the family moved to Missouri in 1818. They settled in Franklin then upon the death of his father through malaria, his mother moved to Arrow Rock in Saline County and opened an elementary school. George, prior to school age, drew on whatever surface available. He apprenticed as a cabinet-maker in Boonville with a man who also was a Methodist preacher. George considered both ministry and law, but his abilities in portraits enabled him to make a living as a painter in 1833 in St. Louis. He studied art in Philadelphia and Europe and then turned to landscapes, focusing on life on the Missouri River.

In 1848, Bingham entered the Missouri State Legislature representing Saline County. He was a dedicated Whig. He served as the Secretary of the Treasury of Missouri during the Civil War from 1862 to 1865. He was appointed the first professor of art at the University of Missouri in 1875. He died in Kansas City.

Joan Nagel died in 2010. Paul Nagel died in 2011 of pancreatic cancer in Edina, Minnesota. Shortly before his cancer was discovered Paul agreed to revise his Missouri history, but it was not to be. My friend still lives through his erudite efforts to map Missouri history.

---

[4] Paul C. Nagel, *George Caleb Bingham: Missouri's Famed Painter and Forgotten Politician*, (Columbia: University of Missouri Press, 2005).

Raftsmen Playing Cards" (1847) by George Caleb Bingham. Saint Louis Art Museum.

114

21
Carry A. Nation (1846-1911): The Hatchet Wielding Missourian

Carry A. Nation (born Carrie) employed the symbol of a hatchet to depict the quest of her life. She actually wielded a hatchet to wreak havoc on alcoholic establishments. She achieved national recognition for her efforts to close down establishments selling alcohol through her rampant attacks. She launched her crusade against alcohol because her first husband, the love of her life, died from a bout with alcoholism. Nation worked both with and independently of the American Women's Christian Temperance Union, founded in 1874 which became significant under the leadership of Francis Willard  (1839-1898) of the Chicago area. Both WCTU and Carry A. Nation are credited with cultivating the grounds for the 18th Amendment to the constitution in 1919, "The Prohibition of Liquor in the United States." During her long crusade Nation was jailed and fined many times for slashing saloons. Nation designated her attacks "hatchetations." She was a strong, six-foot tall woman.

Carrie Nation was also an ordained minister of the Christian Church (Disciples of Christ) as was her second husband, David A. Nation. She was essentially a Charismatic, being open to God speaking to her directly. In the 1890s she announced that she was baptized by the Holy Spirit prompting the Disciples of Christ to disfellowship her in 1892. Nation legally changed the spelling of her name from Carrie to Carry in 1893, because she professed to hear God quoting Jeremiah, "See, I have this day set thee over the nation and over the kingdoms, to root out, and pull down, and destroy, and throw down, to build, and to plant" (Jeremiah 1:10). Carry interpreted this charge to be her own ministry, declaring that she was destined to "Carry A. Nation for Prohibition." Nation was fearless in her attacks because she believed she was carrying out God's will.

For several years, Carry A. Nation was memorialized at Silver Dollar City in Branson, Missouri. An actress depicted her in a parody, "The Saloon Show." In the middle of the skit, the actress stomped on stage brandishing a hatchet, scattered the actors, and broke up the show.

Missouri Times

Nation was born Carrie Amelia Moore in 1846 in Garrard County, Kentucky, south of Lexington. In 1854, the Moores, anticipating the impending Civil War, moved to Belton, Missouri, south of Kansas City. In 1862 in the midst of the war, they moved to Texas, but were back near Belton in 1863. Because of the war, they were forced to move to Kansas City. Carrie as a teenager traveled with another woman to Independence, Missouri and helped nurse wounded soldiers after a skirmish there. In 1867 when the war was over Carrie was 21, and the Moores returned to the Belton, Missouri, farm. Carrie met Charles Gloyd, who was once Moore's boarder, in Belton and they married in November. Charles was a physician who fought in the Civil War. Carry was unaware that Charles had a drinking problem, and after becoming pregnant she realized that he couldn't support her, so she returned to the Moore farm. In 1869, Charles died. Carrie's father had given her land, so she sold the land as well as her husband's book and medical equipment and bought a small house in Holden, Missouri, southwest of Warrensburg. Carrie lived in Holden with her mother-in-law and attended the Normal Institute in Warrensburg for a year—now the University of Central Missouri. She obtained a teaching certificate at the school and taught in Holden from 1872 to 1876. Upon being released from her teaching position, Carrie met and married David Nation, a widower with children, and nineteen years older. He was a journalist for a Warrensburg newspaper, but also a lawyer and later a Disciples of Christ preacher. For at time Carrie managed a hotel in Columbia, Missouri, then moved with Nation to Texas and stayed for ten years. David practiced law and Carrie managed a hotel in Richmond, Texas, southwest of Houston.

In 1898, David Nation accepted the ministry of the Disciples of Christ congregation in Medicine Lodge, Kansas, southwest of Wichita toward Oklahoma. While there, Carrie received a vision that pinpointed her future efforts.

> On the 5th of June, 1899, before retiring, I threw myself face downward at the foot of my bed in my home in Medicine Lodge. I poured out my grief and agony to God, in about this

106

strain: "Oh Lord you see the treason in Kansas, they are going to break the mothers' hearts, they are going to send the boys to drunkards' graves and a drunkard's hell. I have exhausted all my means. Oh Lord, you have plenty of ways. You have used the base things and the weak things, use me to save Kansas. I have but one life to give you, if I had a thousand, I would give them all, please show me something to do." The next morning I was awakened by a voice which seemed to be speaking in my heart, these words, "GO TO KIOWA," and my hands were lifted and thrown down and the words, "I'LL STAND BY YOU." The words, "Go to Kiowa,' were spoken in a murmuring, musical tone, low and soft, but, "I'll stand by you," was very clear, positive and emphatic. I was impressed with a great inspiration, the interpretation was very plain, it was this: "Take something in your hands, and throw at these places in Kiowa and smash them." I was very much relieved and overjoyed and was determined to be, "obedient to the heavenly vision." (Acts 26:19).[1]

Kiowa is a town thirty miles south of Medicine Lodge on the Oklahoma border.

The Crusade

This was the beginning of Carry's crusade. She undertook similar destructive episodes in Wichita and Topeka. These forays interfered with the Nation marriage, and Carry and David divorced in 1901. Nation then started editing first, *Smasher's Mail,* and then *The Hatchet.* She published an autobiography, and from it made enough money with what she already had to open a home in Kansas City to shelter the wives and mothers of drunkards.[2]

At the beginning of the second decade of the twentieth century, Carry became ill. She purchased a house in Eureka Springs, Arkansas, large enough for herself and several women who were homeless because of alcoholic husbands. She insisted that "Men are nicotine-soaked, beer-besmirched, whiskey-greased, red-eyed devils."

Carrie died in Eureka Springs while giving a lecture. She was buried beside her mother in the cemetery in Belton, Missouri. For some time,

---

[1] Carrie A. Nation, *The Use and Need of the Life of Carrie A. Nation.* Revised Edition, 1905. Public domain.

[2] Carry Amelia Nation, *The Use and Need of the Life of Carry A. Nation.* (Topeka: Steves, 1905, 1908).

because of her impoverishment, her grave went unmarked, but the Women's Christian Temperance Movement provided the funds for an impressive stone monument on which are carved the words: "Faithful to the Cause, She Hath Done What She Could."

22

H. Richard Niebuhr (1894-1962): A Major Missouri Theologian

The two most famous Missouri theologians were brothers: Reinhold Niebuhr (1892-1971) and H. Richard Niebuhr (1894-1962). They can be identified as Missourians because they were born in Wright City, fifty miles west of St. Louis on I-70, and educated at Eden Theological Seminary in Webster Groves, Missouri. Reinhold is still extolled for his political theory and ethics. Their sister Huldah (1889-1959) was, for her last 15 years, a professor of Christian Education at Mc-

Cormick Theological Seminary in Chicago. The Niebuhr's were the children of Gustas Niebuhr, a German immigrant Pastor, and his wife, Lydia, daughter of a German Evangelical Pastor.

Early Years

The Missouri area where H. Richard was born was inhabited by German immigrants and their descendants. Regional towns included Wentzville and Hermann. Gustas Niebuhr was a Pastor of the State Prussian

Wright City Town Hall.

Church Union in Germany. Lydia was the daughter of a German Evangelical Synod of America Pastor. This Synod united with the Reformed Church of the United States in 1934, and in 1957, the Evangelical Reformed Church united with the Congregational Christian Church to form the United Church of Christ. The roots of the Congregational Christian Churches were the New England Puritans. Richard attended area schools until 1902 when, at age 8, his father took a pastorate in Lincoln Illinois. Richard entered Elmhurst College, a German Evangelical college in the west Chicago suburbs, graduating in 1913. He returned to Missouri and entered Eden Theological Seminary in Webster Groves, graduating in 1915.

Eden Theological Seminary, Webster Groves. Photo by Tyler Burrus. Copyright Eden Seminary.

Eden Theological Seminary has been a conventional theological graduate school since 1850. It was founded by the German Evangelical Synod of North America in Marthasville, Missouri, on the Missouri River, fifty-five miles west of St. Louis. In 1883, the seminary moved to Webster Groves, a southwest St. Louis suburb, and has functioned there since. H. Richard obtained an M. A. degree from Washington University in 1918 and taught at Eden from 1919 to 1922. He obtained a Ph.D. at Yale in 1924, and after three years as president of Elmhurst College, returned to Eden Theological Seminary as dean from 1927 to 1931. In 1932, he accepted a professorship at Yale and lectured there for thirty years until his death in 1962.

Helmut Richard Niebuhr married Florence Marie Mittendorf in 1920 and had two children, Cynthia and Richard Reinhold, named for his father and uncle. Richard Reinhold Niebuhr (1926-2017) became a professor at Harvard Divinity School in 1956 and remained there his whole career.

I was a student at Harvard Divinity School 1959-62. I took two courses from Professor Niebuhr, one, "Introduction to Theology" and the other, "The Theology of Friedrich Schleiermacher." During that period I heard H. Richard Niebuhr present a lecture at Harvard Divinity School on Christ and Culture.

Helmut Richard Niebuhr was widely recognized for his courses and book on *Christ and Culture* (1951). He explored the disjunction between the transcendent God and the persisting dissonances in human religions and their surroundings. He declared that the means of bridging the chasm was a faith in the one God and the acceptance of personal responsibility to create a context in which unanimity prevailed. Niebuhr questioned the ability of conservative doctrine to overcome the gulf, as well as liberal theology's social activism. He characterized contemporary fragmentation in an earlier work *The Social Sources of Denominationalism* (1929). Niebuhr offered a twofold typology difference between a church and a denomination. A church is composed mostly of lower class, less educated people, and is critical of the ongoing culture. The church type is small, personal, and perfectionistic. A denomination is made up of those better educated, more affluent, and is inclined to accommodate its endeavors to its context. As churches climb the socio-economic ladder, they become denominations.

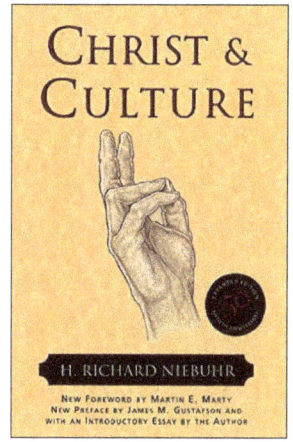

Niebuhr published his most famous book *Christ and Culture* in 1951. He set out five ways different churches relate to culture. First, is Christ against culture which occurs when Christianity hews out a position within a pagan world? Second, is Christ of culture in which the believer affirms that the Spirit of God permeates the natural world? Third, is Christ above culture in which the church through law, reason, and gospel prepare Christians for an ultimate communion with God? In the fourth instance, Christ and culture exist in a paradoxical relationship. Human history is perceived as being on a dual track which consists of faith and unbelief. Faith results in an abundant life which anticipants a new life beyond the grave. The fifth approach is Christ transforming culture. Faithfulness transfigures the present so much so that a fullness of life is realized here and now. Those holding this perspective give less attention to a future transformation beyond time.

Niebuhr spent a year in Basel, Switzerland in 1930, attending the lectures of Karl Barth, considered by many the premier theologian of the twentieth century. Barth led a theological turn to Neo-Orthodoxy focused on the older doctrine of sin and divine grace. Barth criticized social and economic idealism and the Neo-Orthodox theologians concentration on God rather than humanity. H. Richard Niebuhr observed that liberal theology declared "A God without wrath brought men without sin into a kingdom without judgment through the ministrations of a Christ without a cross."

At Yale Divinity School, Niebuhr helped many students prepare for the Christian ministry and teaching. He permitted his students to challenge his theological insights, and his flexibility helped them envisage one God who maintains peace and justice in his universe. Niebuhr avowed that God is above the universe and that all history is under his control. God demands human beings to treat others with dignity and justice. Niebuhr's greatest aspiration was to highlight how humans, communities, and individuals should relate to God and to the world.

Helmet Richard Niebuhr died in 1962 at age 67. He is buried in the Central Burial Grounds in Hampden, Connecticut. Many books have since been written regarding his theology and ethics. H. Richard's statement about pilgrims is an appropriate epitaph.

Pilgrims are persons in motion passing through territories not their own, seeing something we might call completion, or perhaps the word clarity will do as well, a goal to which only the spirit's compass points the way.

23
Mickey Owen (1916–2005): A Missourian's Miscue Remembered

Mickey Owen, born in Nixa, Missouri, south of Spring-field, was a widely recognized major league baseball player, later owner of the Mickey Owen baseball camp in Miller, Missouri, and sheriff of Greene County, Missouri. Mickey was a "golden glove" catcher, but his claim to fame resulted from a passed ball in a Dodger-Yankee game that allowed the Yankees to go on and win the World Series in 1941.

Mickey Owens
trading card.

It seems humiliating to be constantly noted for a mis-cue, but Owen took it stoically. When asked if the error bothered him, Mickey responded: "I would've been completely forgotten if I hadn't missed that pitch." Mickey was correct in his assessment in that at his death obituaries appeared not only in the *Springfield News-Leader*, but also in the *New York Times* and the *Los Angeles Times*. Each of these lengthy obituaries featured the passed ball. Artifacts from this event are preserved at the Baseball Hall of Fame, Cooper-stown, NY.

Owen only committed four errors in 1941 as a catcher for the Brook-lyn Dodgers. The Yankees and the Dodgers competed in the 1941 World Series. At the start of game four, the Yankees held a 2 to 1 Series lead. In the top of the ninth, the Dodgers led 4-3. With two outs, Tommy Hen-rich came to bat and the count went to 3-2. Tommy swung at a wide-ranging curve and missed. The game should have been over and the Se-ries 2-2. But Owen flubbed the ball, and it ended up at the backstop. Owen was unable to throw Henrich out at first base. In the remainder of the ninth, the Yankees scored four runs and won the game. The next day the Yankees beat the Dodgers 3-1 and took the Series.

Mickey Owen's Missouri forebears were farmers, and when not farm-ing, were employed in law enforcement. Three of his relatives served as sheriff of Green County. Mickey Owen lived in Nixa until he was seven when his parents divorced. His mother moved to Los Angeles and took

Mickey along. Mickey played baseball in high school in California, started playing semi-professional ball at fourteen, then returned to Nixa to help with the farming. He also played baseball in a circuit in Arkansas. At age 19, in 1935, he was signed by the St. Louis Cardinals as an amateur free agent. His first assignment was with the Springfield Cardinals of the Class C Western Association. The next year he played at Columbus, Ohio, at the AA level with the Red Birds. Five players on the team were born in Missouri, but Mickey was the only one not born in either Kansas City or St. Louis. He received high marks as a catcher and batted .336. Mickey impressed the Cardinal officials, and in 1937 he moved to St. Louis, playing with several of the famous 1934 World Series-winning "Gashouse Gang." His record at St. Louis, however, was not as impressive, and in 1940 he was traded to the Brooklyn Dodgers. His record with the Dodgers was such that he was elected to the All-Star roster four times from 1941 to 1944.

At the end of the 1945 season, as World War II wound down, Owen served in the navy. He was discharged in 1946 and expected to return to Brooklyn, but could not reach an agreement with the Dodger organization. At that time, the owners of the Mexican league were offering big salaries to players from the United States, and several, such as Max Lanier and Sal Maglie, crossed the border. Mickey Owen accepted a position as player-manager at Vera Cruz in the Mexican League. Baseball management in the United States was incensed, and mandated that players who "jumped" to Mexico could not play in the United States big leagues for three years.

In the summer of 1947, Mickey Owen and several other baseball players barnstormed Missouri and surrounding states, playing local teams. They came to Thayer, Missouri, where I grew up. The game was played on a public field southwest of our small farm. I went down to watch. I don't recall much about the game other than the fact that the famed Mickey Owen was the catcher. When I spoke about the game to my friend Bob Friedman (who also grew up in Thayer) and my good friend, Gail Hopkins (a former major leaguer with the White Sox, Royals, and Dodgers), Bob said that he played in that game. He said when he came up to bat, Mickey told him what each pitch was going to be as the pitcher wound up. Mickey was something of a character.

After the three year penalty, Owen played for the Chicago Cubs from 1949 until 1951. He then managed in the minors and ended his baseball career with the Boston Red Sox in 1954. He served as a Red Sox coach for two years and worked as a scout for the Cubs.

114

The Mickey Owen Baseball School

In 1959, Mickey Owen bought property in Miller, Missouri, on Route 66 west of Springfield where he founded the Mickey Owen Baseball School. He sold the school in 1963, but remained as an instructor even while serving as Sheriff of Green County. The school attracted widespread attention, and prominent alumni included Michael Jordan, Joe Girardi, and Charlie Sheen. The School is now designated "Sandlot Baseball."

Gail Hopkins, a former major leaguer (Kansas City Royals, 1971-1973), had this to say about the Baseball School.

> I think he [Owens] initially sold it to a group of people, but by 1967-68, Phil Rizzo was the majority owner...I was involved with the school on and off from the winter of 1968. Phil lived in Oakbrook, IL but regularly was in Miller during the summer. As I recall, the camp had about 7 graded playing fields, and a number of them had lights so the boys could play at night. There were cabins where the boys would stay and a big central room for food, meeting, games, etc.
>
> Various major league ballplayers would be brought down on days off for the MLB from Kansas City and St. Louis. They would get paid an appearance fee... Sometimes, while I was in med school as I recall in the early 1970s, I bought the school and was the owner of record for one year. The school was sold back to Phil's oldest son who opened other branches in subsequent years.[1]

Green County Sheriff

In 1964 Owen ran for Green County Sheriff. He won four consecutive terms in the office or sixteen years, bowing out in 1981. He became well-known throughout the county. Gail Hopkins wrote,

> I remember once when I was visiting the School, Mick asked me if I liked to hunt. He was an avid hunter, especially birds. I said sure, but not recently. Whereupon, he asked what kind of shot-gun I had. I told him, and he said that it was terrible. We got in

---

[1] Email from Gail Hopkins to Olbricht.

his squad car and drove to Springfield, all the time talking about baseball. I wasn't sure what we were doing, but he was a gregarious fellow, so I went along for the ride. He stopped in Springfield at a sporting goods store and said come on in. He walked in and greeted the proprietor who was behind a long counter with a couple hundred guns along the wall. Mick walk about halfway down the counter, told the proprietor to hand him that 12 gauge Browning on the wall—which the fellow did. Mick looked at it and said put it on my tab, and as we walked out the door, he said: "Now you got a good gun for birds!"[2]

Gail Hopkins had other ties with Missouri. From 1973 to 2006, he owed a farm in Chillicothe.

Owen thought, in the late 1970s, that he had enough political currency to achieve higher office. He ran for Missouri Lieutenant Governor in 1980 and received 13% of the votes in the Democratic primary, but finished third.

In his later years, Mickey Owen developed Alzheimer's disease and lived in a Veteran's Home in Mount Vernon, Missouri, until his death at 89. For 64 years, he was excoriated by Brooklyn fans, but never forgotten.

---

[2] Email from Gail Hopkins to Olbricht.

24
James Cash Penney (1875-1971): Missouri Mogul Milkman

JCPenney is immediately recognized as a major department store chain. Most will presume that the founder was a man named J. C. Penney. Few know that James Cash Penney grew up in Missouri, and in later life owned eight Missouri dairy farms totaling 8,000 acres. Penney was a principal supporter of the University of Missouri's agricultural research, focused on dairy herds and milk production. One manifestation of his philanthropy is the University's Foremost Dairy Research Center located halfway between Columbia and Boonville, Missouri.

Hamilton, Missouri Upbringing

James Cash Penney was born on a farm near Hamilton, Missouri, forty-five miles east of St. Joseph, in September 1875. His father farmed 390 acres and was a Baptist minister who placarded the Golden Rule and emphasized self-discipline and education. The family struggled to make ends meet. While still farming, the family moved into Hamilton, a town with a population of about a thousand, so their children could attend Hamilton High School. Jim, as a growing boy, did farm chores and attended school. By the time he was eight, his father insisted that he earn enough money to buy his own clothes. He proceeded to raise hogs and cattle to accumulate the needed funds. In 1893, J. C. graduated from Hamilton High School with hopes of becoming a lawyer. Not long after, Penney's father died, but he had arranged for Jim to work as a store clerk at the J. M. Hale and Brothers dry goods store in the town. J. C. labored diligently as a salesman and succeeded both in the store and on the family farm.

The Turn to Merchandizing

In 1897, Penney became aware of a persistent illness. The doctors concluded that he was highly susceptible to tuberculosis and recommended that he move to a drier climate. Penney opted for Denver, Colorado, and secured a position in a dry goods store. After a time he bought a butcher shop, but it failed because J. C. refused to provide gratis alcohol to a major customer. In 1898, Penney went to work for a chain in Colorado and Wyoming, called Golden Rule Stores owned by Thomas Callahan and Guy Johnson. Callahan grew to respect Penney and sent him to Evanston, Wyoming, in the southwest corner towards Salt Lake, to work in their Golden Rule store.

Callahan next asked Penney to join the partnership and open a new store in Kemmerer, Wyoming, which Jim proceeded to do. Penney moved there with his new wife, Bertha Alva Hess, and a young son in 1902. Kemmerer was a major coal mining community. In its official history, JCPenney designated the 1902 Kemmerer store as the founding location for the Corporation. The store was one of those in the Golden Rule chain that Penney bought out in 1907. In 1909, Penney moved the headquarters to Salt Lake City, and in 1913 changed the name to J. C. Penney. Penney hired several employees, involved them in the ownership, and designated them "associates," a term he employed from then on. In 1914, J. C. moved the headquarters to New York City. Penney founded his 500th store in Hamilton, Missouri, the town of his birth, in 1924. In the next five years, Penneys expanded rapidly and by 1929 operated 1200 stores. JCPenney had ups and downs over the years and at its height claimed above 2000 locations. The placement of the stores went from smaller towns to the downtown of large cities, and in the 1970s, to shopping malls. James Cash Penney remained on the corporate board until his death in 1971 at 95.

Missouri Farms

We turn now to J. C. Penney's involvement in Missouri agriculture. Penney not only controlled eight farms in Missouri with a total of 8,000 acres, but he also contributed heavily to agrarian research at the University of Missouri. The University awarded Penney an honorary doctorate in animal husbandry.

I was drawn to Penney's farm enterprises because I focused on agriculture at Alton, Missouri High School in 1943 through 1947. My Uncle, Cleo Taylor, was the Vocational Agriculture Teacher, and I both studied under him and worked on his 1260-acre ranch. He encouraged me to get involved in animal production. At the end of the summer of 1947, I owned two New Hampshire sows and a Hereford heifer that I purchased from my uncle. I also purchased the feed. The sows had a few litters of pigs and the heifer had a calf. When I left Alton for college, I sold off my breeding stock at the Thayer, Missouri livestock auction. The breeding females sold well, so that I managed to make $2,000 from my livestock operations. This amount in today's dollars would be $35,000. By making $2,000 or more, it was possible to apply for an FFA recognition—Missouri State Farmer. I had to take an exam, write an essay and report my expenses and profits from farming. In the summer, I received a certificate from the Missouri FFA organization. I was the first from the Alton chapter to secure this status. I was pleased with this attainment.

After a time of living in New York, and after his second wife Mary Hortense Kimball died in 1923, Penney's health declined. He determined to regain his robustness through getting out in the country. He purchased a farm, which he called Emmadine, north of New York City, and raised horses, cattle, sheep, chickens, and Berkshire hogs. His thoughts, however, turned to milk production.

Penney immersed himself in any activity he undertook. In researching dairy production, he discovered that milk production of cows in America was much lower per cow than in Europe. He therefore set out to establish a top-notch dairy herd and selected Guernseys. These milkers were developed on the Isle of Guernsey in the English Channel in the nineteenth century. Not only were the Guernseys heavy producers—almost 4.5 gallons of milk a day—but their milk was rich in butterfat and protein. To establish his superior herd Penney, beginning in 1921, procured cows and bulls from the best stock around the world. Penney was eager to share his insights with whatever dairymen sought him out, for farmers comprised the largest percentage of Penney's customers across the land.

J. C. Penney not only got involved in milk production he was a great advocate of milk as a health drink. My friend Jack Riehl held major supervisory roles in the J. C. Penney Corporation in Italy and the United States. He often met with Penney for business discussions and meals. Riehl wrote,

I can attest to his love for wholesome milk. During every lunch with Penney, he drank whole milk with his meal and gently admonished me for drinking iced tea.

On one occasion, Mr. Penney was a guest speaker at Temple University in Philadelphia. It was a breakfast meal, and he asked me to get him a vanilla milkshake to drink. The time was 7:30 A. M. After bugging a pharmacist to open his drugstore, I obtained a custom milkshake from the annoyed owner. Mr. Penney thoroughly enjoyed every drop of that milkshake.[1]

A Guernsey cow.

J. C. Penney also pursued beef production. On his father's farm, acquired in the 1920s, and the others he purchased in Missouri, Penney developed significant herds of Aberdeen Angus and Herefords, the former black, rectangular cows, and the latter deep red with white faces. On his old home place, he also bred superior horses and mules, the quality of Missouri mules famous throughout the world. In 1938, Penney launched an annual Field Day to exhibit the stature of the animals bred through his endeavors.

The dairy herd established in New York, "The Foremost Guernsey Association" Penney gave to the University of Missouri in 1952. The Foremost Dairy Research Center of the University of Missouri west of Columbia toward Boonville is still operative and is overseen by faculty and maintained by students and regularly hosts visiting groups. It is a working farm of 820 acres. In January 1954, the University of Missouri College of Agriculture took possession of the 268 Guernsey herd from New York valued at $200,000, $350,000 and cash, and $200,000 from the sale on the New York Emmandine farm. That amount is about $7 million in today's dollars. During the years Penney visited the research center regularly to consult with the faculty regarding ways to improve milk production. He stated to Arthur Ragsdale, Chair of Dairy Husbandry, "Missouri is my native state. I am proud of its College of Agriculture." Penney learned, to his distress, that with most great dairy herds, upon the death of their creators, the cows were sold individually. He received assurance

---

[1] Letter from Jack Riehl to Olbricht.

from Ragsdale that the herd he gave to the University would remain intact.

J. C. Penney died in February 1971 at age 95. His funeral sermon was delivered by Dr. Norman Vincent Peale, a renowned New York clergyman who had become Penney's friend. Joseph Cash Penney is interred in the Woodlawn Cemetery in Bronx, New York.

25

John Joseph Pershing (1860-1948): A Missouri Military Hero

Missouri has had wars and military heroes before and since persons of European descent arrived along the major rivers in the 1760s. Battles with the Sauk-Fox Indians erupted in 1812 when the tribe raided settlers along the Missouri River. Chief Black Hawk surrendered at Fort Crawford (1816-1856) in Prairie du Chien, Wisconsin, in 1832. Lt. Jefferson Davis, later president of the Confederacy, stationed at the fort from 1831 to 1834, was charged with accompanying Black Hawk to St. Louis for incarceration. Wars broke out among and with the Osage Indians in 1837. Civil War battles (1861-65) were fought in most regions of Missouri from the battle of Kirksville just south of Iowa to Wilson Creek in Greene County near

Portrait of John J. Pershing by French painter Léon Hornecker.

Springfield. Battles also erupted in Carthage near the Kansas border and at Fort Benton in Patterson in the east toward the Mississippi River. Missouri is still a state with a military presence foremost: Fort Leonard Wood, between Springfield and St. Louis, and Whiteman Air Force Base, at Knob Noster toward Kansas City from Sedalia.

Early Years

The first Missouri general who achieved international acclaim was John Joseph Pershing. Pershing was appointed Commander of the American Expeditionary Force during World War I in charge of two million men. John J. Pershing was born on a farm near Laclede, Missouri, in Linn

County east of Chillicothe. His father, John Fletcher Pershing, who owned a country store and served as postmaster, was of German descent. When John J. Pershing was fourteen in 1873, a major depression ruined the economy. His father had been buying up Missouri farmlands with bank loans, and since he was unable to meet the payments, lost all the farms except one. The father, as a result, became a traveling salesman.

At fourteen, John J. Pershing was forced to be the take-charge guy in his household due to his father's absence. He supervised the farm as well as pursuing an education. He attended a school reserved for honor students whose parents were frontrunners in the community. Upon graduating in

Truman State University Entrance. Photo by Derhai.

1878, he was unable, for financial reasons, to enter college, so he accepted a teaching position at Prairie Mound in Chariton County just south of where Pershing grew up. Pershing saved his earnings and enrolled in the early 1880s at Kirksville Normal School, founded in 1867, and in 1995 renamed Truman State University. After a time Pershing decided he wanted to be a lawyer and apprenticed with an attorney in Kirksville.

While involved in these educational pursuits Pershing read an announcement regarding an entrance exam for the United States Military Academy at West Point, an hour up the Hudson from New York City. Pershing pondered both the quality and no cost features of a West Point education, decided to take the exam, made the top score, and enrolled at West Point in July of 1882. Pershing struggled as a student, but with sheer determination graduated thirtieth in 1886 out of a class of 77 students. His leadership skills were rewarded by his peers who elected him class president four years in a row.

A Military Career

Upon graduation, Pershing was commissioned a Second Lieutenant on September 30, 1886. He considered various options but decided to enter the army. He was assigned to a troop of the 6th United States Cavalry and sent to Fort Bayard in New Mexico Territory, near Silver City, in western New Mexico, not far from the Arizona border. There he engaged in battles with the Apache Indians. Into the 1890s, Pershing fought Indians in California, Arizona, North Dakota, and Iowa. In 1891, John J. was assigned to the University of Nebraska at Lincoln and named Professor of Military Science and Tactics. He occupied this post until 1895, and at the same time studied at the School of Law, from which he obtained a degree in 1893. In 1895 he commanded the 10th Cavalry Regiment troop of Buffalo, that is, African-American soldiers, and helped deport a large number of Cree Indians to Canada.

Captain John J. Pershing, c. 1902.

Pershing was called to West Point in 1897 as an instructor. He was especially strict, decidedly law-and-order, and soon unpopular with the students who, behind his back , designated him "Black Jack" because of his previous military command. The epithet struck. For the next several years Pershing led troops in major battles. In the Spanish-American War, he was quartermaster of the 10th Cavalry, fought in Cuba, and participated in the surrender at Santiago de Cuba. On being awarded a Silver Star, the commanding officer described Pershing's demeanor as "cool as a bowl of cracked ice." He also held commands in Puerto Rico, the Philippines, and Guam.

In 1905, Pershing married Helen Frances Warren whose father was Francis E. Warren, a Wyoming Republican Senator. With the father-in-law's support, President Theodore Roosevelt arranged for Pershing to be promoted to Brigadier General. In 1909, Pershing was sent to the Philippines, served as Commander at Fort McKinley and governor of the Moro Province. Pershing decided in 1915 to bring his family to the Philippians, but before departure, a fire broke out in the Presidio where they lived near San Francisco and Helen and three daughters were asphyxiated in the fumes. Only a son, Francis Warren Pershing, survived. Two years later, in 1917, Pershing courted and was engaged to Anne Wilson "Nita" Patton the younger sister of George S. Patton, famous later because of the movie "Patton"—the General played by George C. Scott. Scott interestingly entered the journalism program at the University of Missouri and graduated in 1953 with degrees in Literature and Theatre. Because of the World War I separation, the marriage of Pershing and Patton never occurred and neither married after the war.

World War I

General Pershing as Army Chief of Staff.

When the United States entered the war in May 1917, President Woodrow Wilson interviewed Pershing and later that year appointed him General of the National Army. By war's end, Pershing had two million men under his command. Pershing arrived in France in June of 1917. The troops under Pershing participated in major battles, a most important one being the second battle of the Marne, the victory Pershing declared a turning point in the war on the Western Front. Pershing, always the take charge general, insisted that, at Argonne, the Germans surrender unconditionally, countering instructions from the Allied Command. Pershing in his memoirs insisted that the battle of Argonne determined the decision of the Germans to accept the unconditional surrender terms. Historians credited American successes in the war to Pershing's military acumen and strategies, and he became the most celebrated World War I hero.

Relief of John Pershing by Walker Hancock at the Kansas City, Missouri, Liberty Memorial. Photo by Einar Einarsson.

In 1919, the United States army authorized President Wilson to promote Pershing to General of the Armies of the United States, the highest rank possible. Pershing left various legacies including the Pershing boot created for trench occupation in January of 1918, and the Military Police in October of 1918. My uncle, Norval Taylor of Thayer, Missouri, was drafted into the army in 1943 and inducted at Jefferson Barracks south of St. Louis. He was then assigned to the Military Police and stationed at Staten Island a borough of New York City. His job was to visit bars in Manhattan and remove trouble making military personnel. Pershing also established associations for veterans and reserve officers.

John J. Pershing retired from the Army in 1924. He was present in Kansas City in 1921 at the groundbreaking of the Liberty Memorial. Visitors included foreign dignitaries and Vice President Calvin Coolidge as a main speaker.

Pershing died at Walter Reed Hospital in Washington, D. C.

26
Ginger Rogers (1911-1995): An Oscar-Winning Missourian

Ginger Rogers (1911-1995) was born and nurtured (in her early years) in Independence, Missouri. She was inducted into the Hall of Famous Missourians in 2009.

Though Rogers performed in several major theater productions, her foremost claim to fame arose from the many films in which she appeared. She is likely best remembered because of the movies she made with her dancing partner, Fred Astaire. The two made ten films from 1933 to 1949. The ones I especially remember were *Flying Down to Rio* (1933), *Top Hat* (1935), and *Shall we Dance* (1937). I watched the videos replayed on television in the 1950s and 60s. In 1939, Rogers and Astaire danced in *The Vernon and Irene Castle Story*.

Photo of Ginger Rogers from the March 1941 issue of International Photographer.

ry. The last choreography was performed to the tune "Missouri Waltz." Both Ginger and Fred appeared in movies separately. I recall seeing Rogers in *I'll Be Seeing You* (1944), *Stage Door* (1937), *Tom, Dick, and Harry* (1941), and *Once on a Honeymoon* (1942).

Early Years in Independence

Rogers was born Virginia Katherine McMath in Independence, Missouri. Her mother's name was Lelee, born in Independence. She was of the Christian Scientist faith. Lelee was estranged from her husband and fled to Independence to keep away from him. Even then, her husband kidnapped Ginger several times before LeLee finally took him to court. Ginger received her name from a cousin who couldn't quite say Virginia.

Original poster for the film
Top Hat (1935), featuring
Rogers and Astaire

The name was appropriate because Ginger was born with auburn hair. In Hollywood films, she was mostly a blond. Lelee left Ginger in Independence with her parents and traveled first to Hollywood, then New York, in search of jobs as a scriptwriter. She obtained adequate income and sent for Ginger.

In 1918, during World War I, Lelee worked in the publicity department of the Marines and sent Ginger back to her parents in Independence. While in the Marines, LeLee met John Rogers, and in May 1920, when Ginger was almost eleven, John and LeLee married in Liberty, Missouri, north of Independence and the Missouri River. John was transferred to Texas and they, along with Ginger, lived in Dallas and Fort Worth.

At age 14, Ginger, encouraged by her mother, entered a Charleston contest and took top honors. Accompanied by her mother, she started traveling with a troop. When she was fifteen, she appeared in vaudeville acts in such cities as Kansas City, St. Louis, and Chicago. They spent their days on the road until 1927 when Ginger was 17. In those years Ginger learned to sing, act and dance. In 1928 daughter and mother went to New York where Ginger sang in two bands and starred in George and Ira Gershwin's 1930 Broadway hit *Girl Crazy*, singing "But not for Me," and "Embraceable You." The first film in which Ginger appeared in 1930 was *A Night in a Dormitory*. Later that year she had bit parts in *A Day of a Man of Affairs* and *Campus Sweethearts*. She started receiving better roles, and charmed moviegoers in *Gold Diggers* in 1933. Her beauty and voice endeared her to film connoisseurs. Ginger, along with Dick Powell, appeared in the 1933 film, *42nd Street*. In 1934, she starred with Powell in *Twenty Million Sweethearts*, depicting the rising popularity of radio. In 1942, Ginger Rogers was the highest paid Hollywood star. Ginger said,

> I'm most grateful to have had that joyous time in motion pictures. It really was a Golden Age of Hollywood. Pictures were talking, they were singing, they were coloring. It was beginning to blossom out: bud and blossom were both present.

Dancing with Astaire

It was with Roger's co-star dancer, Fred Astaire, that the two became the darlings of the silver screen. Their first film was made in 1933. Though they weren't top-billed, it soon became evident that their vigorous, graceful dancing, and personal chemistry were special. The partners sparkled and were irresistibly attractive. In the movie plots, romance bubbled up effervescently. Choreographer Hermes Pan stated, "…there's never been the same electricity that has happened as when Fred and Ginger danced together."[1] Their "Top Hat" film in 1935

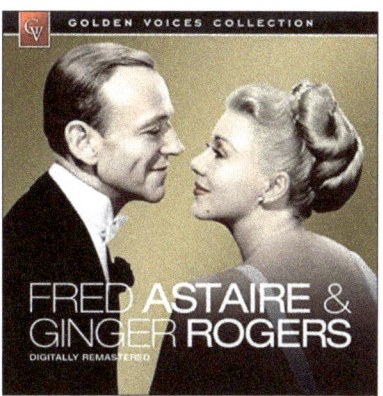

Fred Astaire & Ginger Rogers Cover of *Golden Voices* album.

scored the highest attendance of any in the year. Because of Ginger Rogers' scintillating response to the stately, sophisticated Astaire, a cartoonist, Bob Thaves observed in a famous later line, "Sure he was great, but don't forget that Ginger Rogers did everything he did…backwards and in high heels."[2]

RKO publicity photo of Astaire and Rogers from the film *Roberta*, found in John Mueller, *Astaire Dancing - The Musical Films of Fred Astaire*, Knopf 1985, 67.

Fred Astaire told British TV interviewer Michael Parkinson, when asked about his favorite dancing partner, "I must say Ginger was certainly the one. Everyone knows…I just want to pay a tribute to Ginger because we did so many pictures together and believe me it was a value to have that girl…she had it. She was just great!" In 1946, Ginger wrote about Fred, "I adore the man. I always have adored him. It was the most fortunate thing that ever happened to me, being teamed with Fred: he was everything a little starry-eyed girl from a small town ever dreamed of."

---

[1] Jack Jones. "Master of Style, Elegance Was 88 : Fred Astaire, Movies' Greatest Dancer, Dies." *Los Angeles Times*, June 23, 1987.

[2] From a Bob Staves comic strip, *Frank and Ernest*, in 1982.

An Oscar

The apex in Roger's career arrived in 1940 when Ginger played the lead role in "Kitty Foyle." For her acting skill, she received the 1941 Academy Award Oscar for actress of the year. Over the years she also received several other awards from the Berlin Film Festival, the National Board of Review, the Online Film & Television Association, and has a star on the Hollywood Walk of Fame. In later years, Ginger Rogers owned a ranch in southern Oregon and wintered in Rancho Mirage, California, where a street is named for her.

In *Kitty Foyle*, Ginger played the role of a New York boutique saleswoman who faced the choice of marrying a doctor, Mark Eisen, or running away to South America with Wyn Strafford, a married man she had loved for many years. As she is engrossed in making a decision, she has a flashback to Philadelphia where her blue-collar father cautions her about aspiring to a higher social class. She accepts a position as secretary to the owner of a start-up magazine. The two fall in love, but he is unable to overcome the difference in their class status to marry. Kitty, therefore, moves to New York and takes up her boutique position. She meets Mark Eisen by pretending to faint because she accidentally pushed a burglar alarm. Wyn finally decides to seek her out and they marry. His family scorns Kitty because of her lower-class status, and tells Wyn that if he leaves Philadelphia, he will be disinherited. Kitty decides that divorce is the only option. Kitty next discovers she is pregnant. Wyn seeks her out again, but she refuses to see him when she finds a newspaper story that says he is engaged to someone of his status. The child dies in childbirth. Years later Kitty opens a branch of the New York store in Philadelphia. Without knowing the manager, Wyn's wife enters the boutique. They become acquainted, and Kitty meets the son of Wyn. She gives him an heirloom ring Wyn gave Kitty when they were married. As the film winds down, the plot returns to the present in New York. Wyn reconnected with Kitty and proposed that they leave New York for South America. Though Kitty anguishes over what to do, she decides that her best future lies in marrying Mark, the medical doctor.

Rogers died on April 25, 1995 of congestive heart failure. She was buried side by side with her mother in Oakwood Memorial Park in Chatsworth, California, in the Simi Valley, northeast of Thousand Oaks. Fred Astaire is buried a few yards away.

27

Dred Scott (1799-1858): Freedom Denied by the Supreme Court

In 1857 A Court Case Smoldered in St. Louis; in 1861 Fort Sumter Burned

The name of Dred Scott, an African-American slave, appears in every book on the history of the United States of America. Dred Scott lived in St. Louis, Missouri, most of the years from 1830 until his death in 1858. His last year was his first as a freed slave, but efforts for his freedom had been made since 1846.

Dred Scott and Harriet Scott wood engravings after photographs by John H. Fitzgibbon, St. Louis.

Missouri attained national limelight regarding slavery in 1820 and 1857. Missouri legislators in 1861 were in conflict over whether to secede from the Union. A controversial legislature convened in Neosho and voted to secede. In November 1861, the Confederate Congress voted to admit Missouri as the twelfth Confederate state. But those upholding the decision were forced by federal military action to flee to Arkansas, then to operate from Marshall, Texas. They possessed the state seal, but no real power back in Missouri. Slavery was legal in Missouri until 1865 at the close of the Civil War.

In 1820, Congress passed the famous Missouri Compromise in which Missouri entered the Union as a Slave state and Maine as a Free state. It was a year later, 1821, that Missouri attained official statehood. Congress attempted to keep the balance for the next several years by only approving Slave statehood when paired with a new Free state. The Missouri Compromise decreed that no other state than Missouri was permitted to be a slave state in the Louisiana Purchase north of the "Mason-Dixon" line. This Compromise was rescinded in 1854 with the Kansas-Nebraska Act.

The Supreme Court Decision

According to one Civil War scholar, "The *Dred Scott* case was a major event on the road to the Civil War." The Dred Scott petition for freedom was filed with the United States Supreme Court at the St. Louis County Court House and a decision handed down on March 6, 1957. The ruling was highly dependent on the political climate of the time. Seven of the nine Supreme Court judges were pro-slavery. They declared that Blacks had "no rights which the white man was bound to respect." In addition, they disallowed the right of any territory to prohibit slavery within its own borders, thereby declaring the Missouri Compromise unconstitutional. The decision inflamed antislavery proponents and generated widespread support for the newly formed Republican Party. As anti-slave sentiment accelerated, several slave states seceded from the Union, the Confederacy was born, and the rebels captured Fort Sumter in the Charleston Harbor (South Carolina) in 1861. Civil War erupted across the land.

Dred Scott

Dred Scott was born a slave on the farm of Peter Blow in Virginia in 1795. In 1818 the Blow family moved to Huntsville, Alabama, and continued their agricultural pursuits. In 1830, the Blows moved to St. Louis where they ran a boarding house. Blow sold Dred Scott to John Emerson, a medical doctor. In the early 1830s, Emerson entered the army as a surgeon at Jefferson Barracks. Scott served as Emerson's personal valet. In 1836, Emerson was sent to Fort Armstrong near Rock Island, Illinois. In 1837, the family was transferred to Fort Snelling, on the Mississippi near St. Paul, Minnesota. At Fort Snelling, Dred met and married Harriet Robinson. She was a slave of Lawrence Taliaferro, a justice of the peace, who performed their marriage and sold Harriet to Emerson. In 1838, Emerson moved to Fort Jesup, Louisiana, and the Scotts joined the family, traveling on a Mississippi Riverboat. In 1840, Emerson and his slaves were back in St. Louis. Emerson now leased out the Scotts as household servants. Emerson died, and his widow inherited the Scotts. Dred tried to purchase his family's freedom from Irene Emerson for $300, but she refused. He therefore undertook legal means to obtain his freedom through the St. Louis Circuit Court because he had lived in Free States in Illinois and Minnesota, and therefore, even though he returned to Missouri, by law he couldn't be enslaved again. His legal efforts, however, dragged through the courts for years. Freedom was denied, but with the help of abolitionist lawyers, his case was presented to the United States Supreme Court.

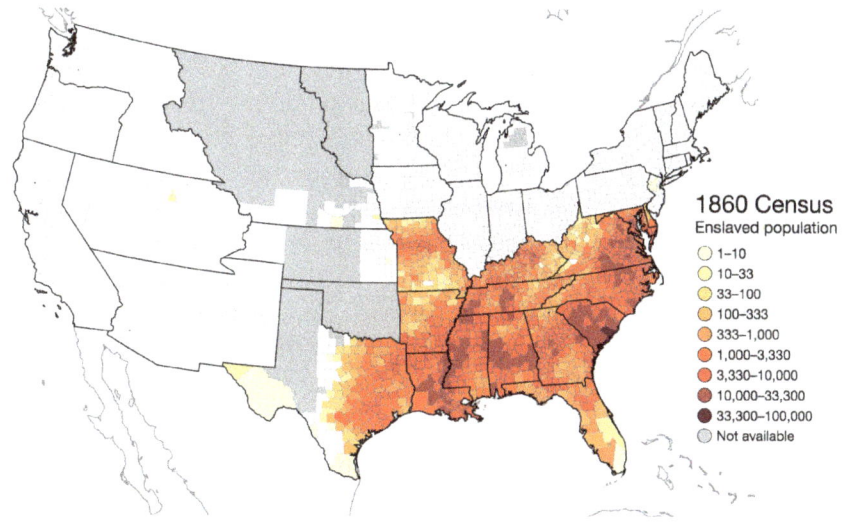

Lincoln Mullen, "The Spread of U.S. Slavery, 1790–1860," interactive map, http://lincolnmullen.com/projects/slavery/, doi: 10.5281/zenodo.9825. Minnesota Population Center, National Historical Geographic Information System: Version 2.0. Minneapolis, MN: University of Minnesota, 2011), http://www.nhgis.org.

African-American Slavery in Missouri

Philippe Renault brought the first African-American slaves to Missouri in 1719. His five hundred slaves came from Santo Domingo Island; were French-speaking and nominally Catholic. They worked in the lead mines west of Ste. Genevieve, and some worked on boats proceeding upstream to St. Louis. In 1830 twenty percent of the St. Louis population consisted of African American slaves. Most slaves worked as stevedores and draymen, on riverboats, in nearby mines, or janitors and porters (like Dred Scott), and as maids, nannies, and laundresses (like Harriet Scott).

In the 1850s, the largest numbers of Missouri slaves were on cotton plantations in the Boot Heel and up the Mississippi as well as on tobacco and hemp farms on the Missouri River from St. Louis to Kansas City. Hemp was grown for its fiber to make rope, paper and cloth, and hempseed oil was burned in lamps. The climate farther north was not suitable for cotton. In 1850, Missouri had 682,044 residents, out of which 87,422 African Americans were slaves and 2618 were free. There were above one thousand African American slaves in only 36 of the 114

Slave auction outside St. Louis County Court House. Court History Museum image.

Missouri counties as the Civil War began. There were almost no slaves in the Missouri Ozarks even on the Arkansas border, a state that seceded to the Confederacy. In the 1930s, no African Americans lived in Oregon County and only a few in West Plains in Howell County. Both counties border Arkansas. "Little Dixie," populated by migrants from Kentucky, Tennessee, North Carolina, and Virginia, had the largest percentage of slaves. Little Dixie bordered on the Missouri River focused on these counties: Callaway, Boone, Howard, Saline, Chariton, Lafayette, and Clay.

The Dred Scott Decision

The efforts of Dred Scott to free his family through the Missouri Courts were long and drawn out. He first tried to buy his freedom from the widow of John Emerson. That failing, in 1847 he filed a case with the state supreme court in St. Louis. He first lost the case on a technicality that he couldn't prove ownership by Emerson's widow. In an 1850 retrial, the Missouri Circuit Court ruled that Scott and his family were free. In 1852, the State Supreme Court reversed the decision. In 1854, the Circuit Court upheld the State Supreme Court. Now the only place to go was the United States Supreme Court. Lawyers and others with anti-slave sentiment encouraged Scott. The case was filed in Washington in 1856 by Roswell Field, the father of Eugene Field, the children's poet. The decision filed in March 1857 once again denied the Scotts their freedom.

Dred and Harriet Scott Statue outside Old Court House, St. Louis.

Through the decade of court cases, Peter Blow's sons encouraged the Scotts by paying their legal fees. After the Supreme Court's decision, these sons obtained ownership of

Scott and his wife and set them free. Scott only lived eighteen months after obtaining his freedom, but his wife lived until 1876, eighteen years later.

28

Henry Miller Shreve (1785-1851): The Steamboat Entrepreneur

Humans began arriving in Missouri perhaps before 20,000 B.C. At one time it was thought that the Carlsbad peoples came first in 13,000 B.C. Now many are convinced that humans crossed the Bering Strait on dry land from Asia, prior to the Carlsbad flint era. The migrants either walked or rode domesticated animals. The first Europeans to visit Missouri came in 1673 and were from French Canada—Jacques Marquette and Louis Joliet. They came by boat and canoe from Lake Michigan, across Wisconsin, and then down the Mississippi. The major ear-

Portrait of Henry Miller Shreve by George D'Almaine, 1808–1892?

ly settlers from the east in the last half of the eighteenth century either came by wagon train beginning in 1781, or flatboats beginning in 1781 from tributaries into the Ohio River and up the Mississippi. It wasn't until the 1850s that many entered the state by railway. My great-grandparents, John Moody and Amy Anthum Waits Taylor, moved to Oregon County, Missouri, in 1869 by horseback and covered wagon from Franklin County in northwestern Alabama. My German-born grandparents Henry and Bertha Lange Olbricht moved to Oregon County, Missouri, in 1910 by train from Crawford, Nebraska, in far northwest Sioux County.

The Steamboat

Another mode of travel was by steamboat. The first steamboat to arrive at the dock in St. Louis was the *Zebulon Pike* in 1817. The first ocean-going steamboat to go up the Mississippi from New Orleans to St. Louis

Drawing of the snagboat *Heiropolis*. Artist unknown.

was *The Washington*, owned by Henry Shreve in 1918. In 1821 a steam boat continued on up the Missouri River to Franklin. The man who made the steamboat the mode of choice until after the Civil War was Henry Miller Shreve. The boats manufactured by Fulton-Livingston were not that suitable for river travel because of the depth of their draft. Shreve engineered a paddlewheel flatboat with a second deck. His boat, which he constantly upgraded, became the standard steamer on the mid-continental rivers.

Furthermore, Shreve invented a special snag boat for clearing obstructions. and received government contracts to work on the major routes, especially the Arkansas and Red rivers ecause he freed the Red river of obstructions, The Louisiana city, Shreveport, was named for him. Shreve traveled by keelboat to St. Louis on the Mississippi as early as 1807. In 1841, Shreve and his family moved to St. Louis, and he lived there until his death in 1851.

Early Years

Henry Shreve was born in Burlington County, New Jersey, East of Philadelphia. In 1788, the family moved to recently founded Brownsville, Pennsylvania, forty miles south of Pittsburgh on the Monongahela River. He ascertained by age fourteen that he wanted to spend his life on the rivers. He purchased his first keelboat in 1807 at age twenty-two, and began a profitable fur trade between Pittsburg and St. Louis. In 1810, he started hauling lead for the Sauk and Fox Indians on the Galena River in Illinois which empties into the Mississippi south of Dubuque, Iowa. He took the lead ingots to New Orleans. He was the first American to take a flatboat that far up the Mississippi.

In 1845, my wife Dorothy's great-great-grandfather Henri Trumpi left Glarus, Switzerland, with a group of almost two hundred immigrants to settle in Wisconsin, supported by the Swiss Emigration Society. After landing in Baltimore, they took a train to central Pennsylvania and from there, steamboats down the Ohio River and up the Mississippi. After a few weeks in St. Louis, they took a steamboat to Galena, Illinois. They traveled by land to Green County Wisconsin, thirty miles south of Madison and founded the town of New Glarus.

After observing the Fulton-Livingston steamboats on the rivers, Shreve concluded that a wider bottom boat was needed. Shreve commissioned the building of *The Enterprise* which was both flatter and wider. He piloted the boat to New Orleans in 1814 and helped Andrew Jackson defend the city in the War of 1812. He then designed *The Washington* that had an ever-shallower hull. With these type boats, Shreve was able to challenge the Fulton-Livingston monopoly on the Mississippi.

Henry Miller Shreve's Steamboat *Washington*. Model by John Bowman.

In 1827, the federal government designated Shreve the Superintendent of Western River Improvements. He designed a special snag boat, *The Heliopolis*, that possessed multiple devices for ramming obstructive trees in the river or hoisting them from the riverbed. The boat even had a sawmill to cut trees into lumber. The United States government appropriated $15,000 to clear the Arkansas River from Pine Bluff to Little Rock and upstream. Shreve contracted for the job and was very successful in clearing the river.

Shreve received special acclaim through removing the Great Red River Raft, consisting of driftwood accumulations in the river segment near Shreveport, Louisiana. The Red River formed the north boundary between Texas and Oklahoma, and runs into the Mississippi and the Atchafalaya Rivers before reaching the Gulf of Mexico. Shreve cleared the Red fifteen miles above Shreveport and eight miles below. Beginning in 1833, he worked on almost two hundred miles of the Red River. Shreve cleared impediments on the streams until 1841 when he lost his post because of an administration change in Washington.

Red River at Shreveport and Bossier City, Louisiana. Courtesy Shreveport-Bossier Convention and Tourist Bureau.

The Move to St. Louis

In 1941, Shreve moved to St. Louis, where he farmed on a plantation he purchased not far from the city. He spent his final years with his daughter Rebecca's family in St. Louis and was buried in Bellefontaine Cemetery in St Louis overlooking the Mississippi River.

In 1986, Henry Miller Shreve was one of the first inductees into the National River Hall of Fame in Dubuque, Iowa, along with Samuel "Mark Twain" Clemens. Shreve was described as "a giant among America's river men and women."

We lived in Dubuque, Iowa from 1955 to 1959. One of our favorite family activities was to drive to Eagle Point Park high on a bluff above the Mississippi River at the north end of Dubuque. After eating a picnic dinner, we walked to the overlook platform and watched the tugboats push multiple barges into the locks about 500 feet below.

The Levee or Landing, St. Louis, Missouri, 1857 from Ballou's *Pictorial Drawing Room Companion.* Unknown artist.

140

The barges and tugs were headed for Minneapolis with gasoline from refineries on the Gulf of Mexico, or going south to New Orleans loaded with cereals from the amber waves of Minnesota grain. All this river traffic navigated past the Missouri riverbanks west of the Mississippi.

Lock and Dam 11 as seen from Eagle Point Park in Dubuque, Iowa. Jun 28, 2006.
Photo by Daniel Callahan.

29
Margaret Truman (1924-2008): The Missouri Legacy of Margaret Truman Daniel

Shortly after the death of Franklin Delano Roosevelt, Harry S. Truman, born in Lamar, Missouri, was sworn in as President of the United States on April 12, 1945. The next day, I climbed up and sat in Truman Raley's, my Alton, Missouri, barber's chair. I was a sophomore in high school. Raley started talking about the new Missouri president. He considered Truman a friendly and competent man. He told me, with pride in his voice, that once when Harry Truman was campaigning for the U. S. Senate, he stopped in for a haircut. Raley then pointed out that I sat in the very same chair in which the president of the United States once sat.

I was aware that many people denigrated Truman. They associated him with the corrupt Kansas City Pendergast machine. They also disdained his populist, plain talk squabbles with his opponents, one of the most famous of which was with a music reviewer who wrote a critical review of the concern singing of his daughter Margaret. Nevertheless, I continued to think kindly of this fellow Missourian.

In 1950 and 1951, I was a member of the Northern Illinois University debate squad. Our debate topic was, resolved "That the non-communist nations should form a new international organization." Because of research for the debates, I learned much about international affairs and concluded that whether or not Truman was a competent president, at least he appointed excellent cabinet members, was not insecure, and depended on their advice. Harry had a plaque on his desk proclaiming, "The buck stops here!" I therefore, despite my roommates' condemnation of Truman for relieving the popular General Douglas MacArthur of his duties in Asia in April 11, 1951, defended Truman's action. In fact, my roommates came back to school after the weekend with a changed point of view. My interest in Truman prompted me to visit his birth home in Lamar, Missouri, drive by his house in Independence, and spend a couple of hours at his "winter White House" in Key West, Florida.

Harry S. Truman House in Independence. Photo by Jack E. Boucher, 1983.

The "Summer White House."

Independence, Missouri

Mary Margaret Truman (1924-2008) was born in Independence, Missouri, named for a grandmother and an aunt. Her parents were Harry S. (a local judge) and Bess Wallace Truman. Margaret attended schools in Independence until 1934 when Harry was elected to the United States Senate. She then divided the time between schools in Independence and Gunston Hall, a boarding school for girls, in Washington. She acted in Shakespeare plays and received honors in English and Spanish. Like her mother Bess, she was not fond of the White House and sometimes referred to it as the Great White Jail. She said she never felt at home there. Young Margaret was drawn to music by her piano-playing father, and he encouraged her to take piano and voice lessons. She received a baby grand piano for her eighth birthday. When she was sixteen, she started taking voice lessons from Mrs. Thomas J. Strickland in Independence.

Margaret wanted to pursue a musical career upon graduating from high school, but her father insisted that she attend college. She entered George Washington University and majored in history and international relations. She almost failed to graduate on time because of a physical education requirement, but she was told that if she swam the length of a 90-foot pool, she would pass. That was a great relief because President Truman gave the commencement address and presented her diploma.

With a B. A. degree in hand, Margaret moved to New York 1946 so as to pursue a singing career. She advanced rapidly, no doubt in part because she was the president's daughter. She made her debut singing with the Detroit Symphony Orchestra on a national radio network in March of 1947. Her first outdoor appearance was at the Hollywood Bowl with 15,000 persons present in August the same year. Eugene Ormandy conducted the orchestra. In December, the president and first lady heard her sing for the first time in person at Constitution Hall in Washington, D. C. Four days later she performed at a concert in Kansas City. She took off time in 1948 to be on the train with her father in his famous "Whistlestop" campaign against Thomas E. Dewey.

Margaret's career continued to advance after she commenced voice lessons with Helen Traubel, who was a Metropolitan Opera star in 1949. In November of that year, she appeared for the first time in Carnegie Hall in New York. Later that month she sang with the National Symphony Orchestra at Constitution Hall in Washington. In the fall of 1950, she sang on a national television show hosted by Ed Sullivan, "The Toast of the Town." She proceeded to make other concert tours from then until 1953, when the Truman's departed from the White House and moved back to Independence. In 1953, she signed a contract with the National Broadcasting Company for singing and hosting shows. In 1955 through 1956 she hosted a radio show, "Weekday." She substituted for Edward R. Murrow in May 1955 for his television program, "Person to Person," and interviewed her parents in their home in Independence.

The Criticism

The controversial defense of Margaret by President Truman occurred in December of 1950 after her concert at Constitution Hall. Paul Hume, music critic for the *Washington Post*, wrote that while he appreciated Miss Truman as a person she didn't sing very well, was sometimes off-key, and the ending was not professional. The President wrote Hume a note in ditch digger language in part declaring, "I have just read your lousy review…I have never met you, but if I do, you'll need a new nose." Truman's aides thought his hasty note was politically a disaster. Interestingly when the mail response to the President's note was opened, eighty percent thought the president was justified. In a 1981 book of Truman family letters, Margaret wrote,

Because of my father, I was more easily able to obtain important engagements. But I also received more attention by first-string critics and more demanding audiences, who felt that because my father was the president, I had to be not better than average, but better than the best in order to justify my appearing on the stage.[1]

Margaret Truman and Clifton Daniel at their wedding. Courtesy Harry S. Truman Library & Museum.

Family

Margaret Truman met Clifton Daniel, assistant to the *New York Times* foreign news editor, in 1955. They married at the Trinity Episcopal Church in Independence, Missouri, on April 21, 1956, when Margaret was 32. She continued to be involved in broadcast media over the next decade of29f and on even though bearing four children: Clifton Truman in 1957, William Wallace in 1959, Harrison Gates in 1963, and Thomas Washington in 1966.

In later life Margaret Daniel kept busy. She continued to work off and on in the media. In the middle 1960s, as the host of the "CBS International Hour," she introduced music and dance programs network officials surfaced from around the globe. She started publishing books including a biography each on her father and mother. The number of books under her name totaled 32, most of which were mystery novels set in Washington, D. C. Many had to do with the federal government, for example, *Murder in the White House*. Donald Bain collaborated with Mrs. Daniel on several of these. In 1984, the city of Independence awarded Margaret the Harry S. Truman Public Service Award presented in the Harry S. Truman Library.

Margaret Truman Daniel and family, Christmas Portrait, 1966. Courtesy Harry S. Truman Library & Museum.

---

[1] Margaret Truman, *Letters from Father: The Truman Family's Personal Correspondence* (South Yarmouth: J. Curley, 1981).

Mrs. Daniel served on several boards. Congress created the Harry S. Truman Scholarship Foundation in 1975. Margaret was appointed to the board in 1977. The scholarships were for college students who anticipated government employment. She was also on the board of the Harry S. Truman Library Institute to support the Truman Library in its educational activities.

Clifton Daniel died in 2000 at age 87. The family had been living in Washington and New York. After her husband's death, Margaret moved to Chicago to be near her oldest son. She died in Chicago in 2008 and is buried in the Harry S. Truman Library and Museum gravesite, beside Clifton Daniel, in Independence, Missouri.

30
Porter Wagoner (1927-2007)
Blond Pompadour Troubadour
Missourian

West Plains, Missouri, in Howell County in the middle of the state on the Arkansas line, has ties with more persons of global renown than any city its size. Dick Van Dyke (1925-) was born in West Plains, Preacher Roe (1916-2008) retired there, and Porter Wagoner (1927-2007) grew up near and in West Plains.

In 1993, I lived in Malibu, California, where I taught at Pepperdine University. One morning I went down to the Malibu Hardware store. As I looked for what I needed, an assistant said to me. "Did you see who came in?" I shook my head. He

Porter Wagoner promotional photo for _The Porter Wagoner Show_ (1961).

continued, "It's Dick Van Dyke." Dick had recently moved to Malibu to launch his television show "Diagnosis Murder." Since seeing celebrities in Malibu is commonplace, I kept looking for my purchase. Then it dawned on me, "Dick was born in West Plains thirty miles from Thayer where I was born. I'll go talk with him." I approached him and spoke of my place of birth. He was very friendly and said he didn't really know much about West Plains since his family moved to Danville, Illinois when he was two. He said what he did know was that the Howell County courthouse burned in the 1930s and he had difficulty obtaining his first passport because the record of his birth was destroyed in the fire.

Preacher Roe was a pitcher for the St. Louis Cardinals, the Pittsburgh Pirates, and the Brooklyn Dodgers. While pitching for the Dodgers, Roe achieved a major record—a 22-3 in 1951. In the 1930s Roe pitched for the Harding College (now University) Bisons in Searcy, Arkansas, and in a 13-inning game struck out 26 batters, and as a result, received national

Preacher Roe Boulevard in West Plains.

attention. Memories of his prowess lingered at Harding when I was a student in the late 40s and later a professor. In retirement, Roe operated a grocery store in West Plains. A section of Highway 160 is named Preacher Roe Boulevard.

Of the three men, Porter Wagoner (1927-2007), spent the most time in Missouri—in West Plains and Springfield. He achieved global fame as a singer of country music. He hosted the Porter Wagoner Television Show on major networks from 1960 to 1981. During that period he recorded several songs with Dolly Parton. Wagoner became a household name with his lofty blond pompadour and colorful rhinestone suits. He wrote numerous songs drawing upon the ballad traditions of his youth. His recording of "Green, Green Grass of Home" created a major sensation and is my favorite among all his recordings. Wagoner is memorialized in West Plains in that US Highway 63 is designated Porter Wagoner Boulevard.

Porter Wagoner was born on a farm southwest of West Plains, near South Fork. Porter, the fifth child, helped on the farm, stacking hay, milking and feeding cows, and slopping pigs. His parents lost the farm because of the depression, and thereupon moved into West Plains in 1943. The family regularly listened to country music, on the radio such as Chicago's National Barn Dance and Nashville's Grand Ole Opry. On the family Victrola, Porter listened to Bill Monroe and the Blue Grass Boys. Wagoner started banging out songs on trees and farm implements, and by the time he was fifteen he owned a guitar, and along with his older brother Glenn, played for area barn dances.

In 1944, at age 17, Porter obtained a job as an assistant in a grocery store, When no customers were present, he plucked his guitar and sang Ernest Tubb and Hank Williams tunes. The owner was impressed with Wagoner's talent, and arranged an early morning radio show on KWMP to promote the store. By 1950, Wagoner had formed a band called The Blue Grass Boys, and they broadcast a show from the butcher shop where Wagoner worked.

Mid-south Missouri was a fertile seedbed for country music. The Grand Ole Opry was conceived by George D. Hay when he came to Mammoth Spring, Arkansas, over the line from Thayer, Missouri, in 1919, to attend a funeral. He heard of a country hoedown the night before on the Missouri border east of Mammoth, which actually may have been in Missouri. When the Opry first aired in 1927, Hay declared that his decision was sparked by that hoedown.

A Thayer Elementary School classmate of mine, John Lewis Mitchell, sang with the Foggy River Boys who were on the Ozark Jubilee and later with different personnel, including John, in Branson from 1973 to 1993. Leroy Chronister, an Alton High (located twenty miles east of West Plains) classmate came from a family of Czech immigrants who played musical instruments and frequented country hoedowns. Chronister was an accomplished fiddler and mandolin player, and recruited another high school student to accompany on a guitar. They played at noon break for thirty minutes in the Alton High gymnasium to a crowd of fifty. Their signature piece was "Down Yonder" (1921).

By 1951, Wagoner had attracted enough attention in the region so that he was invited to Springfield, Missouri, to occupy a fifteen-minute slot of a weekly show on KWTO (Keep Watching the Ozarks). He also traveled the region with a band called the Porter Wagoner Trio with Don Warden on steel guitar and Herschel "Speedy" Haworth on rhythm guitar. They played in school houses and other venues.

In 1955, Red Foley invited Wagoner to join the cast of his Ozark Jubilee. Foley, a veteran star from the Grand Ole Opry, schooled Wagoner in the performing arts and the nuances of rapidly expanding television. Foley came to Springfield in 1955 to host the Ozark Jubilee, which was broadcast on the ABC Network from 1955 to 1960. The Jubilee was renamed The Country Music Jubilee in 1857, and then in 1958, Jubilee USA. Under Red Foley's leadership, the program was the first network production that featured America's top country music stars and thereupon secured a significant international audience. Springfield, for a few years, rivaled Nashville as the capital of country music.

Wagoner played a significant role on the Ozark Jubilee in 1955 and 1956, but then moved to Nashville and joined the Grand Ole Opry in 1957. After his move to Nashville,

Porter Wagoner and Dolly Parton. May, 1969.

Porter Wagoner singing at the Grand Ole Opry in Nashville. Photo ©1999 Larry D. Moore.

Wagoner soared to national prominence and from then on only returned to his home state for short concerts. From 1960 to 1981, he produced the highly successful Porter Wagoner show with globally prominent singers, actors, and instrumentalists. At its peak, the show had 3.5 million viewers. Wagoner was a mainstay on the Grand Ole Opry for a half century. After the death of Roy Acuff in 1992, he became the Opry's unofficial spokesperson. Wagoner was inducted into the Country Music Hall of Fame in 2002.

The Missouri Blond Pompadour Troubadour died from lung cancer in Nashville on October 28, 2007. His music will survive as long as human life endures.

31
Mort Walker (1923-2018): Missouri Creator of Beetle Bailey

Everyone interested in comics remembers Beetle Bailey. Not many, however, can name the comic strip creator—Mort Walker. Fewer still know that Walker had Missouri roots.

Addison Morton Walker (1923-2018) was born in El Dorado, Kansas, thirty miles northeast of Wichita. When

Mort Walker. Image credit BeetleBaily.com

Mort was two, his family moved to Amarillo, Texas. In 1927, when Mort was five, they moved to Kansas City. His father, Robin Adair Walker, was an architect and his mother, Carolyn Richards Walker, a newspaper staff illustrator. Even as a Kansas City elementary school student, Mort drew for the student newspaper. He then attended Northeast High School at 415 Van Brunt Boulevard. Mort was an extremely active high school student. He was a cheerleader, edited the Vikings' newspaper, and was art editor of the school yearbook. He was a high school thespian and a regular participant in a radio drama featured on a Kansas City station. In addition, he ran a teenage center sponsored by several organizations. In his spare time at age 11, he drew and published a cartoon. He sold his first cartoon at 12. By 14 he was regularly selling gag cartoons to *Child's Life,* *Flying Aces,* and *Inside Detective* magazines. At 15, he drew a comic strip for *Kansas City Journal,* a weekly, under the caption *The Lime Juicers.* He also worked on the artist staff of an industrial publisher. Hallmark Brothers was officially launched in Kansas City the year Walker was born, though the organization had an earlier history beginning in 1910 through the enterprises of its founder J. C. Hall. At age 18, Mort was appointed chief designer for the company and changed the Hallmark card motif from cuddly bears to gag cartoons. World War II had begun, and the humorous cards were more in demand by military personnel.

World War II

Upon graduation from Northeast Mort attended what was then identified as the Kansas City Junior College. After a year he enrolled at the University of Missouri. Campus life was cut short in 1943 when Walker, at age 20 was drafted and mustered into the United States Army. When his basic train-ing was completed, he was sent to Italy, which was

Northeast High School Vikings logo. Courtesy Northeast High School.

taken over by the Allies in September 1943. Assigned to Naples, he worked in army intelligence and investigation. He was appointed com-manding officer for an Allied 10,000-German prisoner of war camp. The war ended in Europe in May 1945. Mort continued in the army after the war and was placed in charge of an Italian guard company. In 1947, he was discharged from the army as a first lieutenant.

University of Missouri

Beetle Bailey Statue on the University of Missouri campus.

Walker returned to the University of Missouri to complete his de-gree, and graduated in 1948. He was initiated in the Beta-Gamma Fraternity Chapter before the war and on his return was elected president. He served as editor and art director of the *Showme*, the university humor magazine. His regular visits to "The Shack" for burgers became a part of his mystique. The Shack was located behind Jesse Hall on Conley Avenue. After the creation of Walker's com-ic strip The Shack was frequently mentioned in "Beetle Bailey." In later years when Walker visited the University, he always gravitated to "The Shack," until the building burned in 1988. In 2010, a replica of "The Shack" was constructed in the University student center and officially designated "Morts."

Walker's connection with the University is memorialized by a life-sized bronze statue of Beetle Bailey located in front of the alumni center. Members of the Beta-Gamma Fraternity have alleged that Private Beetle Bailey was modeled after their chapter brothers.

Beetle Bailey and Cartoons

Mort Walker syndicated Beetle Bailey in 1950, two years after graduating from the University of Missouri. As a 50th anniversary celebration in September 2000, the University arranged a major exhibit in the grand concourse of the Elmer Ellis Library with displays of the original daily and Sunday strips along with reprints and poster-sized lithographs of selected cartoons.

Mort Walker's first wife Jean Suffill was also a University of Missouri student, and they married in 1949, not long after Mort left for New York to pursue his comic art career. They met as they both worked on *Showme*. The two had seven children, two daughters, and five sons. The majority of these offspring worked in the Mort Walker enterprises as his career flourished. The couple divorced in 1985 and Mort married Catherine Prentice, who had three children of her own.

Under the impression that New York was the ideal place to pursue his goals, Mort moved there in 1948 and created *Spider*, a *Saturday Evening Post* one-panel series about a lazy, laid-back college student. He soon decided he could make more money with a conventional comic strip and the result was Beetle Bailey, with a new army base setting as opposed to the college campus. The setting was real to Americans with World War II as a recent backdrop and the Korean War constantly in the news. Over several years, the military authorities sometimes banned Beetle Bailey in their publications for fear that a wrong impression was created. Walker had a backlash when he introduced African-American Lieutenant Sonny Fuzz and later Asian Corporal Yo. Eventually, Beetle Bailey was distributed to King Features Syndicated and appeared in 1800 newspapers in more than 50 countries and 200 million daily readers. In later years, Walker received impressive military recognition. In 2000, he was invited to the Pentagon to receive the Secretary of the Army's highest award to a civilian, the Distinguished Citizen Civilian Service Citation. In 1954, Mort and Dik Browne launched *Hi and Lois*, a take-off from Beetle Bailey. He also created several other comic strips, but none were as successful as Beetle Bailey. Through the years he published journals and books.

From 1955 to 1959, I was the debate coach at the University of Dubuque in Iowa. Our 1956-57 debate topic was on a subject in the daily news: "RESOLVED: That the United States should discontinue direct economic aid to foreign countries." I read at least two newspapers a day, sometimes three. I judged that the best information was published in the *Des Moines Register*. I eagerly read the comics and especially looked forward to Beetle Bailey. I started collecting comic books when I was in the third grade in 1937. I had almost complete sets of Superman, Spiderman, Batman, Wonder Woman, and Captain Marvel. They would be worth a fortune now, but they were well worn because they were read by my two brothers and a cousin. I didn't know anything about Mort Walker or that he was a fellow Missourian, but I loved his comic strip.

Mort Walker has been designated the "dean of American cartooning." He was one of the most productive and creative cartoonists in history with nine different strips to his credit. Beetle Bailey turned out to be the most widely syndicated cartoon in the world. In fact, the strip is still being published by Mort's descendants today more than 68 years after it first appeared. Our fellow Missourian holds the record of creating the longest published cartoon—a record that may never be exceeded.

Walker recognized his indebtedness to his alma mater, the University of Missouri, through various bequests. He visited the University of Missouri in 1992 as a Scholar-in-Residence. He gave the University archives numerous artistic creations including original cartoons, animation cels, lithographs, and posters. In addition, the library holds reproductions of Mort's work for the 1946-47 humor magazine *Showme*. Newspaper items about Mort Walker are being added to the collection.

Addison Morton Walker died in Stamford, Connecticut in January of 2018, age 94. He is interred at Willowbrook Cemetery in Westport, Connecticut.

32
Sam Walton (1918-1992): A Major Marketer's Missouri

On April 5, 1992, twenty-six years ago, Sam Walton died of bone cancer at the University of Arkansas Medical Center in Little Rock, Arkansas. Walton was chairman of the board of the fast-growing Walmart Stores, Inc. He was heralded as the wealthiest person in America from 1982 to 1988—worth more than twenty billion dollars at his death. In 2017, the gigantic chain changed its name to Walmart, Inc. signaling its status as a global store and internet merchandizer. In 2018 the company operated in 28 countries and employed approximately 2,300,000 workers (associates), 1,500,000 in the United States.

Sam Walton. c. 1936.

When we recall Sam Walton and place, we naturally think Arkansas. Sam's first retail store in the Benjamin Franklin Five and Ten Chain, purchased in 1945, was located in Newport, Arkansas, ninety miles northeast of Little Rock. Sam and his brother James Bud Walton purchased their second store in Bentonville, Arkansas, in Northwest Arkansas in 1950. The city became headquarters for Walmart, Inc. Their first store designated "Wal-Mart" opened in nearby Rogers, Arkansas in 1962.

Missouri Boyhood

The Walton's, however, had deep Missouri roots. Sam himself lived with his parents in Missouri from 1923 until 1940 when he graduated from the University of Missouri. Sam was born Samuel Moore Walton in Kingfisher, Oklahoma, 50 miles northwest of Oklahoma City in 1918, but his grandfather, Samuel W. Walton (1846-1894), was born in Cooper County, Missouri, in which Boonville is the county seat. Samuel W. Walton's father, William D. Walton (1821-1884), who moved to Missouri, was born in Virginia. Sam's father Thomas Gibson Walton (1893-1984) was born in Diggins, Missouri, east of Springfield. He moved to Kingfisher to farm then to work as a mortgage agent but did not achieve the desired income. Thomas moved the family to Missouri in 1923 when Sam was five years old. The Waltons first settled in Springfield then moved north to Marshall. From Marshall, they moved to Shelbina, 40 miles west of Hannibal. When Sam was in the eighth grade in Shelbina, he achieved Eagle Scout status—the youngest in Missouri history. Sam entered High School in Columbia to which the family had moved, and in 1936 he graduated from the David H. Hickman High School.

Sam was a good student and involved in several high school activities. He was voted the "Most Versatile Boy" by his classmates his senior year. He was the quarterback of the football team, participated in student government, and was elected president of the student body. Because of the family's financial exigencies, Sam earned money in whatever way he could. He sold magazine subscriptions and delivered newspapers. He milked the family cow and delivered the excess milk to neighborhood customers. He sometimes worked in a Five and Ten Cent Store.

Upon graduation in 1936, Walton entered the University of Missouri and signed up for the Reserve Officer's Training Corps (ROTC). He joined the Beta Theta Pi fraternity, where he became an officer, and the Scabbard and Blade Society, a national military honor society. He also became a member of QEBH, a premier secret society founded at the University of Missouri in 1898, honoring the top senior men. He was president of his senior class. He majored in economics.

Sam became a loyal University of Missouri alumnus in later years. He was the recipient of a number of alumni rewards. The University bestowed upon him The Honorary Doctor of Laws in 1984. In 1992, Sam Walton gave $3,000,000 to the College of Business for student scholarships. The funds also established a Sam M. Walton Distinguished Professor of Marketing.

Sam's brother Bud graduated from the Wentworth Military Academy in Lexington, Missouri. When the brothers owned Benjamin Franklin Chain stores, they opened a store in Versailles. Bud and Sam together gave Columbia $150,000 to build the Chamber of Commerce and Convention Center. Bud gave funds to the University of Missouri and to the College of the Ozarks at Point Lookout, Missouri. His daughter, Nancy Walton Laurie of Versailles, gave the University of Missouri twenty-five million dollars to help build their sports arena along with several other grants.

After Sam graduated from Missouri, he took a position with the J. C. Penney Corporation and was sent to Des Moines, Iowa. He received personal instruction from J. C. Penney himself, who grew up in Hamilton,

Missouri, fifty miles east of St, Joseph. After a time of working at an Oklahoma chemical factory, Sam entered the United States Army and was head of security at military bases in the United States.

The Stores

The first Missouri store the Waltons opened in their Benjamin Franklin Chain in 1954 was in the Kansas City Ruskin Heights Shopping Center. The first Wal-Mart stores were opened in Sikeston and Carthage in 1968, and Lebanon, West Plains, and Neosho in 1969. Stores were opened in Joplin in 1971, and Springfield and Columbia in 1973. The first Super Center Wal-Mart opened in Washington, Missouri. in 1988. Sam Walton piloted his own plane and determined to locate sites for new Wal-Marts from the air. The first such site located and purchased was near Fort Leonard Wood.

A Conversation

In 1983, Wal-Mart announced the dedication of a new major store and a refurbished older one in Abilene, Texas. The news release mentioned that Sam Walton would be present for the opening. No private university president could by-pass an opportunity to entertain a prospective donor such as Sam Walton. The president of Abilene Christian University, William J. Teague, host-

Courtesy Walmart Corporate, Bentonville, USA.

ed a luncheon for Sam Walton and fifteen university administrators. I was Dean of the College of Liberal and Fine Arts. Before the luncheon, I introduced myself to Sam and told him I was a Missourian. I observed that he graduated from the University of Missouri. He responded that he had basically grown up in Northern Missouri. We talked about the University. I told him that I was admitted to the University of Missouri to study agriculture in 1949, but decided to finish my college degree elsewhere. I pointed out that Missouri was especially noted for its journalism department. In fact a decade later, the editor-owner of *Missouri Life*,

Danita Wood, held the Meredith Chair and Professor of Journalism at the University from 1995 to 2005. Sam said he knew of the department's reputation. He told me that he had majored in economics. I told him that two of my mother's sisters and two brothers took courses at the University of Missouri in order to qualify to teach vocational home economics and vocational agriculture in Missouri high schools. As far as I know, however, Abilene Christian didn't receive any funds at that time from Sam Walton.

Sam Walton, a major American merchandizer, possessed a bounteous Missouri legacy.

33
Laura Ingalls Wilder (1867-1957): Wilder's Farm in Mansfield, Missouri

Almanzo and Laura Ingalls Wilder moved to a farm in Mansfield, Missouri, 50 miles east of Springfield, in 1894. Laura became famous as the author of a nine children's book series *Little House on the Prairie*, 1932-1943 and 1971. All of these books were published after Laura was sixty-five. The Wilders lived in Missouri from 1894 until their death. Almanzo died in 1947 and Laura in 1957. The Wilders were involved in farming from their early years even before purchasing the Rocky Ridge farm near Mansfield. All the nine children's books were about farms elsewhere than in Missouri: the first four in Wisconsin, New

Laura Ingalls Wilder, c. 1885.

York, Kansas, and Minnesota. The setting for the last five is De Smet, South Dakota, 100 miles northwest of Sioux Falls. Laura makes little reference to Missouri in her books, though there are mentions in volumes not in the series (for example, *A Little House Traveler* written in 1915, but not published until 1974).

Missouri provided an appropriate location for writing books on farm life. As the twentieth century approached, almost three-fourths of Missouri residents lived in rural settings. Even in 2017, Missourians had almost 100,000 farms, second only to Texas. Missouri has a national reputation for breeding of top quality mules. What Missourian, as a teenager, didn't hear from an adult, "You are as stubborn as a Missouri mule"?

Laura Ingalls Wilder (1867-1957)

Laura Ingalls Wilder and her husband, Almanzo Wilder, c. 1885.

Laura Ingalls was born near Pepin, Wisconsin, on the Mississippi 80 miles down-river from Minneapolis, an area of small rolling hill farms. Her father Charles pursued agriculture and other jobs and regularly moved from Wisconsin, first to Rothville, Missouri, a hundred miles north and somewhat west of Boonville, living there in 1869 and 1870. They next moved to Minnesota, then Kansas and back to Wisconsin, then to Iowa often homesteading. One persistent indelible memory in the 1870s was plagues of Rocky Mountain locusts that blackened the sky in the middle of the day and devoured the crops. The Ingalls were among those on the western plains who suffered severe losses from these voracious insects. The swarms finally dissipated in 1902. In 1879, when Laura was twelve, her father took a railroad construction job in De Smet, South Dakota. They continued to live there when Laura married Almanza in 1885. They moved from place to place in a covered wagon. Charles bought or built log cabins, sod dugouts, shanties, and little frame houses for their dwellings in the various locations.

Laura continued her schooling in De Smet, and in 1883 secured her South Dakota teaching certificate. In December she started teaching. She also worked part-time as a seamstress. She made clothes for her own family and quilted from scraps. She attended to the fires, cooked, and stuffed pallets with straw. Laura was not enamored with teaching, but the Wilders needed the money. Laura met Almanzo Wilder when she was fifteen, who was ten years her senior, in De Smet. He grew up in Malone, New York, and raised horses. He owned one of the finest team of Morgans in town. He courted Laura by taking her on buggy rides. Laura insisted on waiting until she was eighteen to marry in 1885. They had a daughter Rose a year later named for the wild prairie flower.

In 1888, Laura and Almanza came down with diphtheria. Almanza had a stroke which forced him to walk with a cane the rest of his life. In 1890 and 1891 the Wilder's moved to Spring Valley, Minnesota, just south of Rochester. Then, in hopes of improving Almanzo's health, they moved to Westville, Florida, but were bothered by the humidity. In 1892 they were back in De Smet where Almanzo worked at various jobs and Laura became a dressmaker. They saved money to purchase a farm.

Farming in Missouri

In 1894, the Wilders moved to Mansfield, Missouri, and bought a 40-acre farm for $100. Through the years they bought more land until they had a sizable farm of 200 acres. They first sold wood, then developed orchards and raised grains to feed chickens, pigs, and dairy cattle. They had ups and downs, but with hard work they managed to survive.

Almanzo Wilder and Laura Ingalls Wilder's Rocky Ridge Farm, Mansfield. Photo by TimothyMN.

A Writing Career

In 1911, Laura commenced writing for the *Missouri Ruralist Magazine*, which is still published. She first wrote bi-weekly articles and then also became editor of the Home Section under the name A. J. Wilder. These articles are for farm women and exhibit Wilder's determination to embrace whatever happens with energy and resolve. Her optimism challenged others to persist, be contented, and make do with what is available. These sentiments are the focal points most often expressed in Laura's essays. Laura also offered practical recommendations in such articles as "Economy in Egg Production," "So We Moved the Spring: How Running Water Was Provided in the Rocky Ridge Farm Home," and in "Shorter Hours for Women," highlighting the use of newly developed electrical devices.

Rose Wilder Lane

A major question among the authorities on the life of Laura Ingalls Wilder is to what extent did the Wilder's daughter Rose Wilder Lane influence the *Little House on the Prairie* series? Rose was born in South Dakota in 1886, and was eight when the Wilders moved to Mansfield. She was educated in Mansfield and stayed with an aunt in Crowley, Louisiana, to receive her high school diploma in 1904. She learned to be a telegrapher in Sedalia in 1905 and then worked for a Kansas City hotel in 1906. Considering job opportunities limited in Kansas City, in 1908 she moved to San Francisco and became a newspaper reporter. Before long she became an assistant at the San Francisco *Bulletin* as well as writing a column that attracted a significant readership. She married Gillette Lane, but they separated in 1915 and later divorced. Laura spent several weeks with Rose in 1915, and they worked on Laura's manuscripts. From 1928 to 1938, Rose returned to Mansfield and lived with her parents.

The writing desk where Laura Ingalls Wilder penned many of the books in her "Little House" novels remains in her former home near Mansfield. Photo by Mark Schiefelbein, AP, 2007.

The years Rose spent in Mansfield were depression years, and she, as well as her parents, lost most of their savings. During the years Rose lived in Mansfield, Laura wrote and published the *Little House* series. Some biographers of Laura claim that Laura's series was essentially ghostwritten by Rose. Pamela Smith Hill of the Missouri State University, Springfield, who has published two books on Laura, acknowledges Rose's editing, but concludes that Rose's contribution was much like that of other editors of the period and while significant, most of Laura's prose remains in the books. Rose became an author of consequence herself, and by 1938 she had adequate income to buy a farm in Danbury, Connecticut, where she lived until her death in 1968. In 1928 Rose built a native Ozark rock house on the farm for her parents and bought her father a Buick. After living in the Rock House for a few years, the parents returned to the frame dwelling and Almanza wrecked the Buick.

"Little House on the Prairie" received international acclaim because of a television series by the same name. The series commenced in 1974 and continued until 1983 with 204 episodes. Michael Landon played Almanzo Wilder and Melissa Gilbert played Laura. It was said to be a favorite Ronald Reagan production.

Dorothy and my children were born in 1952, 1954, 1956, 1958, and 1970. They were readers and loved the "Little House on the Prairie" books. The youngest, Erika, was the right age to become addicted to the television series.

The Wilder farm in Mansfield currently has 50,000 visitors a year. The Wilder estate, with proceeds from the books and television series, is worth one hundred million. Combating the vicissitudes, diseases, and downturns early in life with dedication and hope reaped rewards for Laura and Almanzo beyond their fondest dreams. They are Missourians memorialized!

Rock House residence of Almanzo and Laura Wilder in 1930s. Photo by Billy Hathorn.

34

Harold Bell Wright (1872-1944): A Foremost Romantic Missourian

"The rocks, hills, valleys, streams and trees in the Ozarks are all preachers and they are the kind that do not backslide. There is a good sermon in each one."
—Harold Bell Wright

In 1908, one hundred and ten years ago, an anticipated book arrived at the post office in Branson, Missouri, titled *The Shepherd of the Hills*. It was a romantic novel situated in the hill country around Branson and drew upon the lives of people from the region. It was both applauded by residents, but also denounced as not truly characteristic of Ozark life in the valleys along the White River. In 1941, thirty-three years later, Hollywood produced a major film called "Shepherd of the Hills" starring the inimitable John Wayne. Some of the scenes were shot around Branson, and the film came out in technicolor—a first for John Wayne. In 1960, 58 years ago, Mary Trimble and her son Mark created an outdoor amphitheater on the Lizzie McDaniel estate and started producing a "Shepherd of the Hills" drama with a cast of above a hundred, mostly locals. The "Shepherd of the Hills Outdoor Drama Homestead Park" commenced a new season in the summer of 2018.

Though the best seller *Shepherd of the Hills* survives in book, movie, and drama, Harold Bell Wright (1872-1944) has disappeared in the fog of yesteryear. This, his second novel, sold over a million copies—the first to attain that vaunted number in the United States. Wright's book, *The Winning of Barbara Worth* sold over seven million copies. It is estimated that his nineteen novels sold above 10 million copies and, along with income from movies, made Wright a millionaire. Harold Bell Wright was a Christian Church (Disciple of Christ) minister before he was an author of nineteen romances. Wright set out to be neither a preacher nor a novelist.

The Early Years Before Missouri

Harold Bell Wright was born near Rome, New York, east of Syracuse, on the heralded Erie Canal. His father was a ne'er-do-well drunk, and the family moved from town to town. His mother died when Harold was eleven. His father sent the children to relatives and to whoever would care for them. Harold wandered through the region finding what work he could, often sleeping in the woods and outbuildings. He worked as a sign painter, a house painter and an artist. He painted a sign for an evangelistic tent meeting in Grafton, Ohio. Intrigued, he attended the gathering. He was impressed, and before the series was over, he had talked with the Christian Church minister and was baptized, thus becoming a member of that alliance.

Wright was studious, though he did not have the level of education that qualified him for college. Grafton was near Oberlin, Ohio, southwest of Cleveland. From the Grafton members, he heard about a Disciples' College in Hiram, Ohio, southeast of Cleveland. In 1893, he entered the preparatory school at Hiram to prepare to enter the college. In 1895, he enrolled in the college, but never completed his degree since he developed breathing problems that afflicted him the rest of his life. He was sometimes on the verge of tuberculosis. The first college classes were held at Hiram in 1867. James A. Garfield, later a United States President, was head of the earlier-launched preparatory school from 1856 to 1859.

The Christian Church (Disciples of Christ)

The Christian Church (Disciples of Christ) grew out a movement to restore New Testament Christianity. Early leaders were Barton W. Stone (1772-1844) of Kentucky and Illinois, and Thomas (1763-1854) and his son Alexander Campbell (1788-1866), both born in Northern Ireland and who later immigrated to Bethany, West Virginia, in the early 1800s. By 1900 the churches of this persuasion had a million members in the United States.

Before the Civil War, especially in "Little Dixie" around the Missouri River west of Jefferson City, Christian Church members were in the majority north of the Missouri River. In the early twentieth century there were four Disciples Colleges in Missouri: Culver-Stockton College in Canton, founded in 1853, Drury University in Springfield, founded in

1873 and connected with the Christian Church in 1909, Columbia College in Columbia in 1851, and Williams Woods University in Fulton in 1870. James Shannon, a Christian Church minister, who earlier administered at Columbia and Culver-Stockton, was president of the University of Missouri from 1850 to 1856.

Wright as a Christian Church Preacher

When Harold Bell Wright, because of respiratory problems, departed from Hiram College, relatives suggested that moving west might improve his health. His uncle Ben lived near Springfield, Missouri, and proposed that he move to that region. Wright relished walking in the Ozark hills, streams, and flora and his health improved. While living in Mt. Vernon,

Christian Church in Pierce City.
Courtesy of Dave Hadsell.

Missouri, Wright was invited to preach a sermon at the Christian Church in Pierce City, Missouri. He accepted the invitation and preached metaphorically from the broken branch and leaf of a tree. He was invited back and then offered the position as pastor for the congregation. He moved to Pierce City and worked there from 1896 through 1898. He was remembered by the congregation, and the old building in 1933 became the Harold Bell Wright/Pierce City Museum.

Wright left Pierce City and moved to Pittsburg, Kansas, northwest of Joplin, to serve as minister to the Pittsburg Christian Church. While in Pittsburg he married Frances Long in 1899. He was in Pittsburg from 1898 to 1903 and wrote his first published novel, *That Printer of Udell's*. The book was first offered serially in the denomination's journal, *Christian Century*, based in Chicago. Wright was not overly pleased with the novel, but some of his members read it in the *Christian Century* and proposed that he read it to the congregation which he proceeded to do on Sunday nights. A few years earlier Charles Sheldon read his unpublished book, *In His Steps* (1896), with the famous question, "What Would Jesus Do?" on Sunday nights to his congregation in Topeka, Kansas. Wright's book was published in 1903 and had enough sales for Wright to contemplate his next book—*Shepherd of the Hills*.

The moving of ministers every two or three years was typical in Christian Churches at the turn of the century. The Wrights next moved to Kansas City (1903-1905) where Harold preached for the Forest Avenue Christian Church. For Wright, this congregation was too large and the expectations too demanding. He next accepted a call to the Christian

Church in Lebanon, Missouri, where he preached from 1905 to 1907. While there he worked on *The Calling of Dan Matthews* (1909) and Lebanon (Corinth in the novel) was the setting. Wright also wrote much of *The Shepherd of the Hills* in Lebanon. He spent considerable time around Branson in summers: fishing, hunting, camping, and hiking.

Because of persistent health problems, Wright accepted a call to the Christian Church in Redlands, California, southeast of San Bernardino, where he served beginning in 1907. At that point, he decided to retire from the ministry and devote full time to writing. He concluded that he was more effective getting his message across by writing than from the pulpit. Through his novels, he was able to interject applied Christianity into the conflicts between good and evil among working-class people.

My mother, the incurable reader, loved the novels of Harold Bell Wright. She liked him because of his romantic plots and his religious values. Our church background was the same as that of Wright. She encouraged me to read his novels, and I read a few when I was eleven to thirteen. I'm sure I read *Shepherd of the Hills* and *The Winning of Barbara Worth*.

In 1908, Wright and his family moved to the Imperial Valley of California, east of San Diego. He bought a ranch between El Centro and Holtville, not far from Mexicali, Mexico. Because of respiratory problems he moved to Tuscan, Arizona, in 1915. In 1935, he moved to the

San Diego area, buying an estate in Escondido. He died in the Scripps Hospital in La Jolla in 1944. Through all these years, Harold Bell Wright continued to write and to help prepare ten of his novels for filming.

For those into sleuthing, telltale signs of Harold Bell Wright can still be located wherever he lived. But the place where his life's work is best memorialized is in Branson, Missouri.

Shepherd Inspiration Tower, Branson, Missouri.

Index of Places

Index of Names

About the Author

Thomas H. Olbricht was born in Thayer, Missouri, and lived in Thayer and Alton from 1929-1947. He has received degrees from Northern Illinois University, University of Iowa, and Harvard Divinity School. Pepperdine University conferred the DHL on Olbricht in 2011. Olbricht has taught at Iowa, Harding, University of Dubuque, Penn State, Abilene Christian, and Pepperdine, and has written and or edited twenty-five books, including Missouri Memories 1934-1947. His ancestors have lived in Missouri since 1850 and obtained degrees from Missouri State and the University of Missouri. Olbricht has taught Pepperdine Off-Campus Graduate courses in the Red Bridge area of Kansas City.